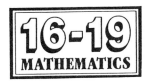

Matrices

The School Mathematics Project

The right of the
University of Cambridge
to print and sell
all manner of books
was granted by
Henry VIII in 1534.
The University has printed
and published continuously
since 1584.

Cambridge University Press

Cambridge   New York   Port Chester   Melbourne   Sydney

Main authors	Simon Baxter
	Stan Dolan
	Doug French
	Andy Hall
	Barrie Hunt
	Lorna Lyons
Team leader	Barrie Hunt
Project director	Stan Dolan

The authors would like to give special thanks to Ann White for her help in preparing this book for publication.

Cartoons by Paul Holland
Illustrations by Andy Hall

Published by the Press Syndicate of the University of Cambridge
The Pitt Building, Trumpington Street, Cambridge CB2 1RP
40 West 20th Street, New York, NY 10011-4211, USA
10 Stamford Road, Oakleigh, Melbourne 3166, Australia

First published 1991

Produced by Laserwords and 16-19 Mathematics, Southampton

Printed in Great Britain by Scotprint Ltd., Musselburgh.

ISBN 0 521 42651 0

Contents

1 Introduction to matrices

1.1 Data storage

There are many instances where information is presented in the form of a two-way table.

Injuries in 18 tobogganing accidents. Four accidents resulted in two separate injuries.

Type of accident	Type of injury			
	Facial injury	Soft tissue	Fracture	Head injury
Collision with obstacle	2	2	3	1
Fall on slope	6	1	1	2
Collision with another person	2			2

BMJ Vol 302 6 April 1991

Such a table is called an array of data, or a **matrix**. (Note: the plural of matrix is matrices).

Several examples of the use of matrices are shown below.

- A bus timetable has rows representing the times of departure from a particular stop, and columns representing the journey of each bus.

Mon - Sat										ROUTE 308
	dep	dep	dep		dep	dep	dep	dep	dep	arr
Abbey Road	0615	0645	0715	then	1945	2015	2115	2215	2315	2344
Bill's Garage	0622	0652	0722	every	1952	2022	2122	2222	2322	- - -
Cinema	0626	0656	0726	30 mins	1956	2026	2126	2226	2326	- - -
Dockside	0632	0702	0732	until	2002	2032	2132	2232	2332	- - -
Empire Hotel	0637	0707	0737		2007	2037	2137	2237	2337	- - -

- The matrix below shows how many direct routes there are between each pair of stops served by the bus company.

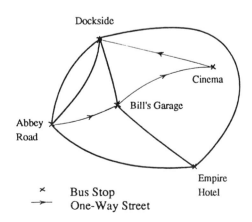

From

		A	B	C	D	E
	A	0	0	0	2	1
	B	1	0	0	1	1
To	C	0	1	0	0	0
	D	2	1	1	0	1
	E	1	1	0	1	0

✗ Bus Stop
→ One-Way Street

1

- Water supplies in some areas are found to have very high levels of certain pollutants. One way to reduce the level of a particular pollutant supplied to individual houses is to mix water from a number of different areas. For example, by combining water from a rural reservoir containing a high concentration of nitrates with water from a densely populated area whose main pollutant is bacteria, the resulting mix contains safe levels of both.

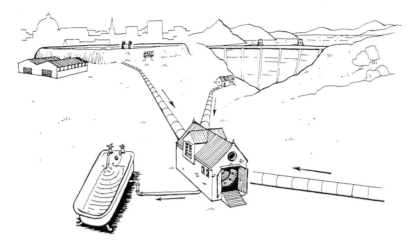

The proportions of water supplied by reservoirs A, B and C to pumping stations α, β and γ are shown in the following flow network and matrix.

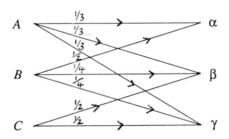

		From		
		A	B	C
	α	$\frac{1}{3}$	$\frac{1}{2}$	0
To	β	$\frac{1}{3}$	$\frac{1}{4}$	$\frac{1}{2}$
	γ	$\frac{1}{3}$	$\frac{1}{4}$	$\frac{1}{2}$

- The matrix shown below represents a household budget, produced on a spreadsheet.

	1990				
	1st quarter	2nd quarter	3rd quarter	4th quarter	Total
Cash	1000	1000	1000	1000	4000
Fuel and telephone	350	270	220	300	1140
Car and petrol	300	430	150	280	1160
Food	470	470	470	470	1880
Mortgage	1600	1600	1600	1600	6400
Local tax	200	200	200	200	800
Clothes	180	50	200	100	530
Standing orders	750	820	790	910	3270
Total	4850	4840	4630	4860	19180

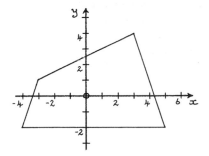

Reading clockwise, the quadrilateral has coordinates

$(3, 4)$, $(5, -2)$, $(-4, -2)$, $(-3, 1)$

These points can be shown in a matrix with the coordinates forming the columns

$$\begin{bmatrix} 3 & 5 & -4 & -3 \\ 4 & -2 & -2 & 1 \end{bmatrix}$$

If the coordinates are always written the same way round, there is no need for row/column headings.

An American-style fast-food outlet in Moscow sells soft drinks in three sizes - small, medium and large. The prices, in copecks (100 copecks = 1 rouble) are shown in the following matrix

	S	M	L
Cola	36	40	44
Root beer	42	47	52

or $\begin{bmatrix} 36 & 40 & 44 \\ 42 & 47 & 52 \end{bmatrix}$

If you always write the drinks and the sizes in the same order it becomes unnecessary to label the matrix. Even if the prices are changed, the position in the matrix specifies the drink.

This matrix has 2 rows and 3 columns, so it is referred to as a **2 x 3 matrix**.
2 x 3 is the **order** of the matrix.
Each entry in the matrix is called an **element**.
Suffix notation is used to refer to a particular element. For example, in a matrix **A**, the element in the 2nd row and 3rd column is a_{23}. In the matrix above, this represents the price of a large root beer.

An hour's sales of soft drinks at one cash till are given by the matrix

$$\mathbf{B} = \begin{bmatrix} 9 & 12 & 11 \\ 3 & 7 & 2 \end{bmatrix}$$

(a) How many medium colas were sold ?

(b) What information is given by the element b_{21} ?

(c) Evaluate $\displaystyle\sum_{i=1}^{2} \sum_{j=1}^{3} b_{ij}$

What information does this represent ?

3

1.2 Matrix arithmetic

One advantage of storing information in matrix form is that it allows calculations to be carried out in an efficient way.

 TASKSHEET 1 - *Matrix arithmetic*

Matrix arithmetic

2 x 2 matrix addition is defined as

$$\begin{bmatrix} a_{11} & a_{12} \\ a_{21} & a_{22} \end{bmatrix} + \begin{bmatrix} b_{11} & b_{12} \\ b_{21} & b_{22} \end{bmatrix} = \begin{bmatrix} a_{11} + b_{11} & a_{12} + b_{12} \\ a_{21} + b_{21} & a_{22} + b_{22} \end{bmatrix}$$

2 x 2 scalar multiplication is defined as

$$k \begin{bmatrix} a_{11} & a_{12} \\ a_{21} & a_{22} \end{bmatrix} = \begin{bmatrix} ka_{11} & ka_{12} \\ ka_{21} & ka_{22} \end{bmatrix}$$

2 x 2 matrix multiplication is defined as

$$\begin{bmatrix} a_{11} & a_{12} \\ a_{21} & a_{22} \end{bmatrix} \begin{bmatrix} b_{11} & b_{12} \\ b_{21} & b_{22} \end{bmatrix} = \begin{bmatrix} a_{11}b_{11} + a_{12}b_{21} & a_{11}b_{12} + a_{12}b_{22} \\ a_{21}b_{11} + a_{22}b_{21} & a_{21}b_{12} + a_{22}b_{22} \end{bmatrix}$$

These results can be extended to $m \times n$ matrices. Matrices are multiplied by multiplying the elements in a row by the elements in a column and adding the results.

$$\begin{bmatrix} \cdot & \cdot & \cdot \\ a_{21} & a_{22} & a_{23} \\ \cdot & \cdot & \cdot \end{bmatrix} \begin{bmatrix} \cdot & \cdot & b_{13} & \cdot \\ \cdot & \cdot & b_{23} & \cdot \\ \cdot & \cdot & b_{33} & \cdot \end{bmatrix} = \begin{bmatrix} \cdot & \cdot & \cdot & \cdot \\ \cdot & \cdot & c_{23} & \cdot \\ \cdot & \cdot & \cdot & \cdot \end{bmatrix}$$

Here $c_{23} = a_{21}b_{13} + a_{22}b_{23} + a_{23}b_{33}$

$m \times n$ matrix addition is the same as for 2 x 2 matrices in that you add the corresponding elements to obtain the new matrix.

Exercise 1

1. $A = \begin{bmatrix} 4 & -2 \\ 3 & 9 \end{bmatrix}$ $B = \begin{bmatrix} -3 & 4 \\ 0 & 3 \end{bmatrix}$ $C = \begin{bmatrix} 2 & 8 \\ -6 & 4 \\ 3 & -1 \end{bmatrix}$ $D = \begin{bmatrix} 5 & 3 \\ 0 & -2 \\ 1 & -7 \end{bmatrix}$

   $E = \begin{bmatrix} 7 & 1 & -8 \\ 12 & -10 & 4 \end{bmatrix}$

   Evaluate

   (a) **A + B**   (b) **C + D**   (c) **7A**   (d) $\frac{1}{5}$ **E**   (e) **AB**

   (f) **CE**   (g) **ED**

2. For the flow network with reservoirs A, B, pumping stations α, β, γ and houses a, b, c:

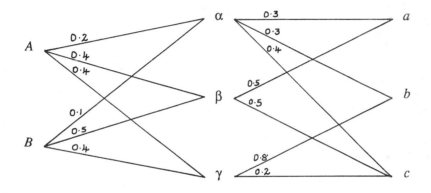

   (a) Write down the flow matrices for

      (i) reservoirs to pumping stations

      (ii) pumping stations to houses.

   (b) Find the rate of flow into the pumping stations if the output from A and B is $\begin{bmatrix} 20 \\ 20 \end{bmatrix}$ litres per second.

   (c) Find the rate of flow into the houses using your answers to (ii).

   (d) Evaluate the matrix representing the flow from reservoirs to houses.

   (e) Use this matrix to verify your answer to (c).

1.3 Properties of matrix arithmetic

Real number arithmetic has various well-known properties. For example, any two real numbers can be multiplied together to give a real number and any two real numbers can be added together to give a real number. There are, however, some pairs of real numbers where one cannot be divided by the other, for example $6 \div 0$.

> (a) **Find two matrices which cannot be added together.**
>
> (b) **Can you find a scalar and a matrix which cannot be multiplied together?**
>
> (c) **Can you find two matrices which cannot be multiplied together?**
>
> (d) **Describe the conditions under which each of the types of calculation described above can be carried out.**

You know that if r is a real number, then $0 + r = r$ and $1 \times r = r$. The next tasksheet compares these and other properties of real number arithmetic with those of matrix arithmetic.

TASKSHEET 2 - *Properties of matrix arithmetic*

For matrices A, B and C:

A + B can be evaluated if A and B are of the same order.

AB can be evaluated if A is of order $m \times n$ and B is of order $n \times p$. The result will be of order $m \times p$.

ASSOCIATIVE LAWS: $\quad (A + B) + C = A + (B + C)$
$$(AB) C = A (BC)$$

COMMUTATIVE LAWS: $\quad A + B = B + A$
In general, $AB \neq BA$

$0 = \begin{bmatrix} 0 & 0 \\ 0 & 0 \end{bmatrix}$ is the identity matrix for 2×2 matrix addition

$I = \begin{bmatrix} 1 & 0 \\ 0 & 1 \end{bmatrix}$ is the identity matrix for 2×2 matrix multiplication

Exercise 2

1. For each of the following calculations, state whether they can be carried out and, for those which can, give the order of the result.

(a) $\begin{bmatrix} 4 & 7 \\ 8 & 1 \\ 2 & 6 \end{bmatrix} + \begin{bmatrix} 3 \\ 1 \\ 2 \end{bmatrix}$

(b) $\begin{bmatrix} 2 & 3 & 2 \\ 4 & 1 & 6 \end{bmatrix} + \begin{bmatrix} 2 & 7 \\ 8 & 1 \\ 3 & 9 \end{bmatrix}$

(c) $\begin{bmatrix} a_{11} & a_{12} & a_{13} & a_{14} \\ a_{21} & a_{22} & a_{23} & a_{24} \end{bmatrix} + \begin{bmatrix} b_{11} & b_{12} & b_{13} & b_{14} \\ b_{21} & b_{22} & b_{23} & b_{24} \end{bmatrix}$

(d) $k \begin{bmatrix} 3 & 1 \\ -8 & 6 \\ 0 & -5 \end{bmatrix}$

(e) $\begin{bmatrix} 2 \\ 4 \\ 7 \end{bmatrix} \begin{bmatrix} 3 \\ 7 \\ 6 \end{bmatrix}$

(f) $\begin{bmatrix} 4 & 8 & 9 & 6 \end{bmatrix} \begin{bmatrix} 2 & 8 \\ 7 & 6 \\ 3 & 2 \\ 1 & 4 \end{bmatrix}$

(g) $\begin{bmatrix} a_{11} & a_{12} \\ a_{21} & a_{22} \\ a_{31} & a_{32} \end{bmatrix} \begin{bmatrix} b_{11} & b_{12} & b_{13} \\ b_{21} & b_{22} & b_{23} \\ b_{31} & b_{32} & b_{33} \end{bmatrix}$

2. For each type of matrix given below, determine whether

(a) the matrices are closed under multiplication;

(b) the operation of multiplication is commutative.

(i) $\begin{bmatrix} 1 & a \\ 0 & 1 \end{bmatrix}$ (ii) $\begin{bmatrix} 1 & a \\ a & 1 \end{bmatrix}$ (iii) $\begin{bmatrix} a & b \\ 0 & a \end{bmatrix}$

1.4   Transition matrices

In section 1.1 you saw how a matrix can be used to represent the flow in a set of pipes. At each stage in the process the output depends upon the input at the previous stage. Now that you have the necessary techniques, this idea will be developed to consider examples of how matrices can represent other situations in which the outcome depends in some way on the preceding state.

As a first example, consider a three stage process in which water is passed through a sequence of pipes as shown:

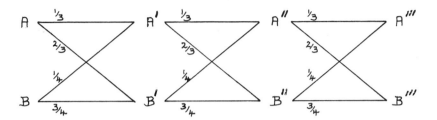

At each stage the proportions of water passing through the pipes are given by the same matrix, for example:

$$\mathbf{T} = \begin{matrix} & A & B \\ A' & \begin{bmatrix} \frac{1}{3} & \frac{1}{4} \\ \frac{2}{3} & \frac{3}{4} \end{bmatrix} \end{matrix}$$

If the inputs at A and B are 100 litres per minute and 200 litres per minute, respectively, they can be represented by the input matrix

$$\mathbf{a} = \begin{bmatrix} 100 \\ 200 \end{bmatrix}$$

(a)   **Explain why the output matrix after the first stage of the process is given by Ta.**

(b)   **What is the output matrix after the second stage in terms of T and a?**

(c)   **What is the output matrix after the third stage in terms of T and a?**

(d)   **If the process were to have n stages instead of three, what would be the output at the final stage?**

The matrix **T**, which defines the output at a given stage in terms of the input to that stage, is known as a **transition** matrix. Transition matrices have a wide range of applications and are particularly important in the fields of genetic theory and population dynamics.

Example 1

A student is sometimes late for classes. If she is on time for class one day, there is a probability of $\frac{1}{3}$ that she will be late the next day. If, however, she is late for class there is a probability of $\frac{1}{10}$ that she will also be late the following day.

(a) Draw a network diagram to illustrate the situation.

(b) On the first day she is on time. Write down the matrices $\mathbf{a}_1$ and $\mathbf{a}_2$ that describe her behaviour on the first and second days.

(c) Write down the transition matrix, $\mathbf{T}$, for the problem.

(d) Write down, in terms of $\mathbf{T}$ and $\mathbf{a}_1$, the matrix $\mathbf{a}_n$ which describes her behaviour on the nth day.

Solution

(a) Let P stand for punctual, L for late. The network is then

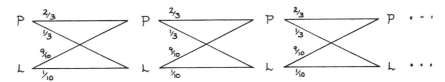

(b) $\mathbf{a}_1 = \begin{bmatrix} 1 \\ 0 \end{bmatrix}$ $\qquad\qquad\qquad$ $\mathbf{a}_2 = \begin{bmatrix} \frac{2}{3} \\ \frac{1}{3} \end{bmatrix}$

(c) It is important here to keep the order of the rows and columns the same as the order of the vectors.

$$\mathbf{T} = \begin{array}{c} \\ P \\ L \end{array} \begin{array}{cc} P & L \\ \begin{bmatrix} \frac{2}{3} & \frac{9}{10} \\ \frac{1}{3} & \frac{1}{10} \end{bmatrix} \end{array}$$

(d) Since $\mathbf{a}_2 = \mathbf{T}\mathbf{a}_1$

$\qquad\qquad$ $\mathbf{a}_3 = \mathbf{T}\mathbf{a}_2 = \mathbf{T}^2\mathbf{a}_1$ etc.,

it follows that $\mathbf{a}_n = \mathbf{T}^{n-1}\mathbf{a}_1$.

A process for which the probability of a subsequent event depends upon the outcome of its preceding event is known as a **stochastic process**.

In order to predict the pattern of behaviour of a stochastic process over several stages it is necessary to be able to evaluate powers of $\mathbf{T}$. Clearly it is not hard to evaluate $\mathbf{T}^2$ and even $\mathbf{T}^3$, but for larger values of n the process will become tedious. A useful technique for evaluating higher powers of matrices is developed in Chapter 4.

Exercise 3

1. On a Saturday night a student either goes to the disco or to the cinema. If he has been to the disco the previous Saturday then there is a probability of $\frac{1}{2}$ that he will go to the disco again. However, if he has been to the cinema the previous Saturday there is a probability of $\frac{3}{4}$ that he will go to the disco.

   (a) Draw a network diagram to illustrate the situation.

   (b) On the first Saturday he goes to the cinema. Write down the matrices $\mathbf{a}_1$ and $\mathbf{a}_2$ that describe his behaviour on the first and second Saturdays.

   (c) Write down the transition matrix, $\mathbf{T}$, for the problem.

   (d) Write down, in terms of $\mathbf{T}$ and $\mathbf{a}_1$, the matrix $\mathbf{a}_n$ which describes his behaviour on the nth Saturday.

2. A tennis player hits either to her opponent's forehand or her opponent's backhand. If she has previously hit to the forehand then she has a probability of $\frac{4}{5}$ of hitting to the backhand on the next shot. If, however, she has previously hit to the backhand there is a probability of $\frac{2}{3}$ that she will again hit to the backhand.

   (a) Write down the transition matrix for the problem.

   (b) If her first shot is to her opponent's backhand, calculate the probability that the third shot will also be to the backhand.

   (c) What is the probability that her fourth shot will be to her opponent's backhand if her first shot is to the

      (i) backhand;

      (ii) forehand?

3. If a day is fine, the probability that the next day will also be fine is $\frac{4}{5}$. If it is wet, the probability that the next day is wet is $\frac{1}{3}$. Write down the transition matrix for the problem and use it to calculate the probability that, if a given day is fine it will also be fine in 2 days' time.

TASKSHEET 3E - *Leslie matrices*

After working through this chapter you should:

1.   be aware of examples of data which may be represented in matrix form;

2.   understand the way in which suffix notation may be used to describe the elements of a matrix;

3.   be able to perform the operations of matrix addition, scalar multiplication and matrix multiplication on compatible matrices;

4.   know the laws of matrix arithmetic and in particular realise that in general $AB \neq BA$;

5.   understand the term transition matrix and apply such matrices to problems involving stochastic processes.

Matrix arithmetic

The fast-food outlet in Moscow described in Section 1.1 sells cola and root beer in three sizes, small, medium and large. The prices, in copecks, are shown in the following matrix:

	S	M	L
Cola	36	40	44
Root beer	42	47	52

The sales in one hour at three of the cash tills are given below:

till 1
$$\begin{bmatrix} 9 & 12 & 11 \\ 3 & 7 & 2 \end{bmatrix}$$

till 2
$$\begin{bmatrix} 3 & 8 & 7 \\ 5 & 4 & 6 \end{bmatrix}$$

till 3
$$\begin{bmatrix} 17 & 12 & 15 \\ 22 & 16 & 11 \end{bmatrix}$$

Matrix addition/subtraction

1. (a) Find the total sales matrix for (i) tills 1 and 2
                                           (ii) all three tills.

    (b) Find a matrix which shows how much better the sales were at till 3 than at till 2.

2. Using the same method as in question 1, work out

    (a) $$\begin{bmatrix} 3 & 4 \\ 2 & 1 \\ 6 & 7 \end{bmatrix} + \begin{bmatrix} 5 & 2 \\ 1 & 7 \\ 3 & 2 \end{bmatrix}$$

    (b) $$\begin{bmatrix} 7 & 5 \\ 8 & 4 \end{bmatrix} - \begin{bmatrix} 2 & 3 \\ 2 & 1 \end{bmatrix}$$

    (c) $$\begin{bmatrix} a_{11} & a_{12} & a_{13} \\ a_{21} & a_{22} & a_{23} \end{bmatrix} + \begin{bmatrix} b_{11} & b_{12} & b_{13} \\ b_{21} & b_{22} & b_{23} \end{bmatrix}$$

Multiplication of a matrix by a scalar

3. What would be the matrix of total sales at till 1 in a 12-hour day if the sales were to continue at the same rate?

4. Using the same method as in question 3, multiply each matrix by the given scalar:

    (a) $$5 \begin{bmatrix} 3 & 2 & 5 \\ 4 & 1 & 3 \end{bmatrix}$$

    (b) $$0.5 \begin{bmatrix} 4 & 3 \\ 1 & 2 \end{bmatrix}$$

    (c) $$k \begin{bmatrix} a_{11} & a_{12} & a_{13} \\ a_{21} & a_{22} & a_{23} \end{bmatrix}$$

(continued)

12

Matrix multiplication

5.   A factory makes three types of radio using three different components.

	Standard	Traditional	De Luxe
Component A	2	1	3
Component B	4	2	1
Component C	2	3	3

The matrix above shows the numbers of each component used in each type of radio. The cost, in pence, of each component is shown below.

$$\begin{matrix} A & B & C \\ [90 & 48 & 73] \end{matrix}$$

Complete the matrices below to show

(a)   How many of each component are needed to make 7 Standard, 12 Traditional and 3 De Luxe radios?

$$\begin{bmatrix} 2 & 1 & 3 \\ 4 & 2 & 1 \\ 2 & 3 & 3 \end{bmatrix} \begin{bmatrix} 7 \\ 12 \\ 3 \end{bmatrix} = \begin{bmatrix} \cdot \\ \cdot \\ \cdot \end{bmatrix} \begin{matrix} A \\ B \\ C \end{matrix}$$

(b)   How much would it cost to make one of each type of radio?

$$[90 \quad 48 \quad 73] \begin{bmatrix} 2 & 1 & 3 \\ 4 & 2 & 1 \\ 2 & 3 & 3 \end{bmatrix} = \begin{matrix} S & T & D \\ [& &] \end{matrix}$$

6.   Using the same method as in question 5, multiply each pair of matrices together.

(a)
$$\begin{bmatrix} 3 & 4 \\ 2 & 1 \\ 6 & 7 \\ 9 & 2 \end{bmatrix} \begin{bmatrix} 5 \\ 1 \end{bmatrix} = \begin{bmatrix} \cdot \\ \cdot \\ \cdot \\ \cdot \end{bmatrix}$$

(b) $[3 \quad 7 \quad 9 \quad 1] \begin{bmatrix} 4 \\ 7 \\ 9 \\ 3 \end{bmatrix} = [\cdot]$

(continued)

13

7. Two reservoirs, A and B, supply two pumping stations, α and β, in the proportions shown:

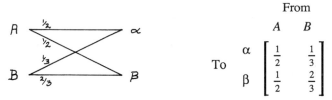

From

To $\quad \begin{matrix} \alpha \\ \\ \beta \end{matrix} \begin{bmatrix} \dfrac{1}{2} & \dfrac{1}{3} \\ \dfrac{1}{2} & \dfrac{2}{3} \end{bmatrix}$

(a) If water leaves reservoir A at a rate of 16 litres per second, and reservoir B at a rate of 9 litres per second,

(i)   what are the rates at which the water arrives at each pumping station?

(ii) Evaluate $\begin{bmatrix} \dfrac{1}{2} & \dfrac{1}{3} \\ \dfrac{1}{2} & \dfrac{2}{3} \end{bmatrix} \begin{bmatrix} 16 \\ 9 \end{bmatrix} = \begin{bmatrix} \cdot \\ \cdot \end{bmatrix}$ What do you notice?

(iii) What rates of flow from the two reservoirs would cause water to arrive at α and β at $\begin{bmatrix} 20 \\ 25 \end{bmatrix}$ litres per second?

(b) Combining the flow from reservoirs to pumping stations to houses a and b gives the network

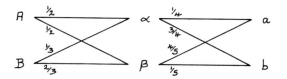

(i)   Complete the flow network to show the proportions of water from each reservoir finally supplied to each house.

Note: $\dfrac{1}{2} \times \dfrac{1}{4} + \dfrac{1}{2} \times \dfrac{4}{5} = \dfrac{21}{40}$

(ii) What is the matrix representing this flow?

(iii) The flow arriving at α and β is represented by $\begin{bmatrix} \dfrac{1}{2} & \dfrac{1}{3} \\ \dfrac{1}{2} & \dfrac{2}{3} \end{bmatrix} \begin{bmatrix} p \\ q \end{bmatrix}$ where p, q are the flows leaving A, B.

Explain why the flow arriving at a and b is represented by

$\begin{bmatrix} \dfrac{1}{4} & \dfrac{4}{5} \\ \dfrac{3}{4} & \dfrac{1}{5} \end{bmatrix} \begin{bmatrix} \dfrac{1}{2} & \dfrac{1}{3} \\ \dfrac{1}{2} & \dfrac{2}{3} \end{bmatrix} \begin{bmatrix} p \\ q \end{bmatrix}$

(continued)

Notice that, in the matrix multiplications of questions 5 and 6, each row in the first matrix was multiplied by the column of the second matrix. This can be extended to multiplying each row in the first matrix by each of several columns in the second.

$$\begin{bmatrix} \cdot & \cdot & \cdot \\ * & * & * \\ \cdot & \cdot & \cdot \end{bmatrix} \begin{bmatrix} \cdot & \cdot & * & \cdot \\ \cdot & \cdot & * & \cdot \\ \cdot & \cdot & * & \cdot \end{bmatrix} = \begin{bmatrix} \cdot & \cdot & \cdot & \cdot \\ \cdot & \cdot & * & \cdot \\ \cdot & \cdot & \cdot & \cdot \end{bmatrix}$$

2nd Row x   3rd Column $\rightarrow$ Element a_{23}

(iv) Evaluate

$$\begin{bmatrix} \frac{1}{4} & \frac{4}{5} \\ \frac{3}{4} & \frac{1}{5} \end{bmatrix} \begin{bmatrix} \frac{1}{2} & \frac{1}{3} \\ \frac{1}{2} & \frac{2}{3} \end{bmatrix} = \begin{bmatrix} \cdot & \cdot \\ \cdot & \cdot \end{bmatrix}$$

(v) Explain why your answers to (ii) and (iv) are the same.

(vi) Use your answer to (ii) to find the rate of water arriving at a and b if the output from A and B was $\begin{bmatrix} 80 \\ 30 \end{bmatrix}$ litres per second.

8.   (a) Complete the following:

(i) $\begin{bmatrix} 4 & 2 & 8 \\ 3 & 3 & 7 \end{bmatrix} \begin{bmatrix} 1 & 4 \\ 6 & 1 \\ 5 & 9 \end{bmatrix} = \begin{bmatrix} \cdot & \cdot \\ \cdot & \cdot \end{bmatrix}$

(ii) $\begin{bmatrix} 3 & 4 \\ 2 & 1 \end{bmatrix} \begin{bmatrix} 2 & 6 \\ 3 & 1 \end{bmatrix} = \begin{bmatrix} \cdot & \cdot \\ \cdot & \cdot \end{bmatrix}$

(iii) $\begin{bmatrix} 4 & 7 & 1 \\ 3 & -5 & 2 \\ -4 & 7 & -3 \\ 0 & 8 & 2 \end{bmatrix} \begin{bmatrix} 8 & 1 & 6 \\ 1 & -3 & -2 \\ 0 & -7 & 9 \end{bmatrix} = \begin{bmatrix} \cdot & \cdot & \cdot \\ \cdot & \cdot & \cdot \\ \cdot & \cdot & \cdot \\ \cdot & \cdot & \cdot \end{bmatrix}$

(b) Explain what happens when you try to evaluate

$$\begin{bmatrix} 4 & 7 \\ 1 & 2 \\ 6 & 5 \end{bmatrix} \begin{bmatrix} 2 & 8 & 1 \\ 0 & 3 & 2 \\ 7 & 5 & 9 \end{bmatrix}$$

15

Properties of matrix arithmetic

Real numbers have several easily verified properties. Using real numbers a, b and c, some of them are illustrated below.

(i)   Associative law of addition: $(a + b) + c = a + (b + c)$

(ii)   Associative law of multiplication: $(ab)c = a(bc)$

(iii) Commutative law of addition: $a + b = b + a$

(iv) Commutative law of multiplication: $ab = ba$

(v)   The identity for addition is 0: $a + 0 = a$

(vi) The identity for multiplication is 1: $a \times 1 = a$

1.   (a)   Choose some values for a, b and c to demonstrate properties (i) and (ii).

        (b)   Explain each of the properties (i) to (vi) in words.

2.   (a)   For 2 x 2 matrices **A**, **B** and **C**, investigate whether properties (i), (iii) and (iv) hold.

        (b)   For each property, either prove that it holds true using the usual suffix notation a_{ij}, or give a counterexample to demonstrate that it is false.

3.   Verify that the associative law holds for an arbitrary pair of 2 x 2 matrices. (It is possible to prove that it holds, but the algebra is very tedious!)

4.   Find 2 x 2 matrices **0** and **I** such that **0** is the identity for 2 x 2 matrix addition and **I** is the identity for 2 x 2 matrix multiplication.

5.   (a)   Is it possible to find two real numbers, a and b, such that $a + b$ is not a real number?
(If no such counterexample exists, then real number addition is said to be closed.)

        (b)   Is real number multiplication closed?

        (c)   Is subtraction closed on the set of positive integers?

        (d)   Is 2 x 2 matrix addition closed?

        (e)   Is 2 x 2 matrix multiplication closed?

(continued)

6. Consider the set S of matrices of the form $\begin{bmatrix} 1 & 0 \\ a & 1 \end{bmatrix}$, $a \in \mathbb{R}$

   (a) Write down any two members of S and find their product. Does this product matrix belong to S also?

   (b) By considering two such arbitrary matrices $\mathbf{A} = \begin{bmatrix} 1 & 0 \\ a & 1 \end{bmatrix}$ and $\mathbf{B} = \begin{bmatrix} 1 & 0 \\ b & 1 \end{bmatrix}$, show that $\mathbf{AB} \in S$ for all members of S. i.e. show that S is closed.

   (c) Is the set of matrices of the form $\begin{bmatrix} 2 & 0 \\ a & 2 \end{bmatrix}$ closed? Justify your answer.

7. Consider the set of 3 x 3 matrices of the form $\begin{bmatrix} a & 0 & 0 \\ 0 & b & 0 \\ 0 & 0 & c \end{bmatrix}$, a, b and $c \in \mathbb{R}$.

   (a) Choose two matrices $\mathbf{A}$ and $\mathbf{B}$ of this form. Evaluate $\mathbf{AB}$ and $\mathbf{BA}$. Are the results of the same form?

   (b) Continue to investigate the closure of these matrices until you have found a counterexample, or else can prove that the set is closed under multiplication.

Leslie matrices

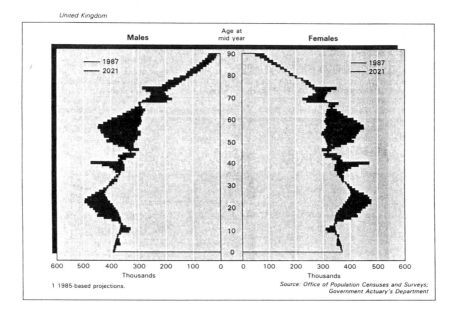

United Kingdom

One of the most important applications of mathematics is to make predictions about the future using data from the past. In social and economic planning it is essential to be able to make detailed predictions, not merely about population growth, but also about changes in age structure. For example, if the country is to build nursery schools and train the right number of nursery teachers it is necessary to have reliable estimates of numbers of under-fives many years before the children who will use the schools are born! Equally, higher education provision, care for the elderly and staffing of maternity wards all need knowledge of numbers in various age strata of the population. An important tool in such planning is a transition matrix, known as **the Leslie matrix.**

The use of Leslie matrices can be illustrated using an example which, although simplified, demonstrates the basic principles. The first simplification is to consider only the population of females and the second is to assume that the population consists of 5 age groups $0-14$, $15-29$, $30-44$, $45-59$ and $60-74$.

1.   Would you expect the age structure of the female population to differ greatly from that of the male population?

The female population (in millions) of the U.K. in 1987 may be described using the matrix

$$\mathbf{p}_0 = \begin{bmatrix} 5.2 \\ 6.6 \\ 5.8 \\ 4.6 \\ 3.6 \end{bmatrix}$$

2.   (a)   How many females were there in the age group $45-59$?

(b)   In order to estimate the age structure 15 years later, what information is required?

(continued)

18

The age structure in the year 2002 can be calculated if the proportion of each generation that survives into the next generation and the numbers that are born during the next 15 years are known. However, the numbers that are born depend, not on the **total** population, but on the **fertile** population and on their respective fertility rates (i.e. the number of children on average that are produced by one female in a 15-year period).

Suppose that these rates are

	0 – 14	15 – 29	30 – 44	45 – 59	60– 74
P (survival)	0.99275	0.99047	0.97366	0.83333	0
fertility rate	0.05885	1.09798	0.13523	0	0

3.   (a)   Why is it necessary to take the probability of survival in the 60 – 74 year group as 0?

(b)   Calculate the number in the age groups

(i)   30 – 44

(ii)   0 – 14

in the year 2002.

If information in the table above is stored in matrix form then it can be readily manipulated and predictions about population can be made.

$$\mathbf{L} = \begin{bmatrix} 0.05885 & 1.09798 & 0.13523 & 0 & 0 \\ 0.99275 & 0 & 0 & 0 & 0 \\ 0 & 0.99047 & 0 & 0 & 0 \\ 0 & 0 & 0.97366 & 0 & 0 \\ 0 & 0 & 0 & 0.83333 & 0 \end{bmatrix}$$

The population matrix $\mathbf{p}_1$ in the year 2002 can then be calculated using the matrix product $\mathbf{L}\mathbf{p}_0$

$$\mathbf{p}_1 = \begin{bmatrix} 0.05885 & 1.09798 & 0.13523 & 0 & 0 \\ 0.99275 & 0 & 0 & 0 & 0 \\ 0 & 0.99047 & 0 & 0 & 0 \\ 0 & 0 & 0.97366 & 0 & 0 \\ 0 & 0 & 0 & 0.83333 & 0 \end{bmatrix} \begin{bmatrix} 5.2 \\ 6.6 \\ 5.8 \\ 4.6 \\ 3.6 \end{bmatrix}$$

$$= \begin{bmatrix} 8.34 \\ 5.16 \\ 6.54 \\ 5.65 \\ 3.83 \end{bmatrix}$$

(continued)

The matrix **L** is known as the **Leslie matrix**

4.   (a)   How would you use the Leslie matrix to estimate the age structure in 100 years time?

       (b)   What assumptions does this involve?

Successive age structures may be calculated using powers of **L**. Thus, if $\mathbf{p}_2$ is the population after 2 generations,

$$\mathbf{p}_2 = \mathbf{Lp}_1 \quad = \quad \mathbf{L(Lp}_0) \quad = \quad \mathbf{L}^2\mathbf{p}_0$$

One important function of population dynamics is to establish criteria for a stable distribution of population. In matrix terms this is equivalent to writing $\mathbf{p}_1 = \lambda\mathbf{p}_0$ because an age distribution similar to that in 1987 would have a matrix proportional to that for 1987. Matrix equations of the form

$$\mathbf{Lp}_0 = \lambda\mathbf{p}_0$$

will be studied in a later chapter.

Further questions

5.   A species that can be divided into 3 age groups has probabilities of survival into successive age groups of 0.9, 0.7 and 0 . The fertility of each group is 1.12, 0.5, 0.1 respectively and its initial population is described by the matrix

$$\begin{bmatrix} 80 \\ 50 \\ 40 \end{bmatrix}$$

    (a)   Write down the Leslie matrix for the population.

    (b)   Use this to predict the population after 2 generations.

6.   In the management of grey seal stocks, the Leslie matrix for the population of the Farne Islands is

$$\begin{bmatrix} 0 & 0 & 0 & 0 & 0.08 & 0.28 & 0.42 \\ 0.66 & 0 & 0 & 0 & 0 & 0 & 0 \\ 0 & 0.93 & 0 & 0 & 0 & 0 & 0 \\ 0 & 0 & 0.93 & 0 & 0 & 0 & 0 \\ 0 & 0 & 0 & 0.93 & 0 & 0 & 0 \\ 0 & 0 & 0 & 0 & 0.935 & 0 & 0 \\ 0 & 0 & 0 & 0 & 0 & 0.935 & 0.935 \end{bmatrix}$$

In this case the age groupings are for one year with all animals over the age of six considered together. (J. Harwood & J.H. Prime, 'Some factors affecting the size of the British grey seal populations' *Journal of Applied Ecology* 15,(1978), 401–11).

Suppose that initially the population is evenly distributed over the age groups. By inventing a suitable initial matrix, comment on the population trend over the next three years.

Tutorial sheet

1. $A = \begin{bmatrix} 2 & 1 \\ 5 & 2 \\ 3 & 7 \end{bmatrix}$ $B = \begin{bmatrix} 4 & 8 & 1 & 5 \\ 7 & 3 & 6 & 9 \end{bmatrix}$ $C = \begin{bmatrix} 3 & 1 & 7 \\ 6 & 2 & 8 \\ 9 & 1 & 2 \\ 4 & 7 & 1 \end{bmatrix}$

   (a) Find the orders of

   (i) **AB**   (ii) **BC**   (iii) **A(BC)**   (iv) **(AB)C**

   (b) By evaluating **A(BC)** and **(AB)C** test the conjecture that the associative law also applies to multiplication of non-square matrices.

2. For real numbers a, b and c,

   $$a(b+c) = ab + ac$$

   This is the distributive law for multiplication over addition.
   Does this equivalent law hold for 2 x 2 matrices?

3. (a) Consider the proof of $(a+b)^2 = a^2 + b^2 + 2ab$ $(a, b \in \mathbb{R})$ by multiplying $(a+b)(a+b)$. Which properties of real number arithmetic (for example commutative law, associative law etc.) have been used?

   (b) Now consider the expansion of $(A + B)^2$ where **A** and **B** are 2 x 2 matrices

   (i) Give a counterexample to show that $(A + B)^2 \neq A^2 + B^2 + 2\,AB$.

   (ii) Explain why the proof that you used for real numbers in (a) does not transfer to matrices.

   (iii) Write down a correct expansion for $(A + B)^2$

   (continued)

4.   In Section 1.1 you saw that the map

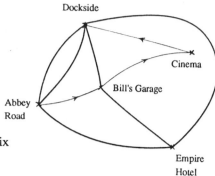

Dockside

Cinema

Bill's Garage

Abbey
Road

Empire
Hotel

can be represented by the route matrix

$$\mathbf{R} = \begin{bmatrix} 0 & 0 & 0 & 2 & 1 \\ 1 & 0 & 0 & 1 & 1 \\ 0 & 1 & 0 & 0 & 0 \\ 2 & 1 & 1 & 0 & 1 \\ 1 & 1 & 0 & 1 & 0 \end{bmatrix}$$

The bus company charges fares according to the number of steps in the journey. The journey from A to E may be made as a two-step journey in 3 ways A - B - E, A - D - E (twice, using the two different routes between A and D).

(a)   Assuming that the different bus routes cover all possible journeys, complete the following matrix to show all the possible two-step journeys $\mathbf{T} = \begin{bmatrix} 5 & . & . & . & 2 \\ . & 2 & . & . & . \\ 1 & . & . & 1 & . \\ . & . & . & 6 & . \\ 3 & 1 & . & 3 & 3 \end{bmatrix}$

(b)   Evaluate $\mathbf{R}^2$?

What do you notice?

(c)   What do you think $\mathbf{R}^3$ will represent?

5.   Between 1955 and 1989 England played 35 Rugby Union internationals against Wales, of which 5 were draws. Excluding draws, the sequence of winning teams was as follows:

        W   W   E   W   E   W E W   W   W   W   W   W   W   W   E   W
        W   W   W   W   E   W E W   W   E W   W   W

(a)   Calculate the probability that if England win in one year, they will also win in the following year.

(b)   Calculate the probability that if Wales win in one year, they will also win in the following year.

(c)   Write down a transition matrix for the problem.

(d)   In 1990 England won. Find the probability for each team to win in 1993.

6.   Find a matrix such that   (a) $\mathbf{M}^2 = \mathbf{I}$ where $\mathbf{M} \neq \mathbf{I}$

                                (b) $\mathbf{M}^2 = \mathbf{0}$ where $\mathbf{M} \neq \mathbf{0}$

2 Matrices and transformations

2.1 Transformations

Geometrical transformations are an important application of matrices. They are used in this chapter to develop some properties of matrices, which will be applied particularly to the solution of sets of equations in the following chapter.

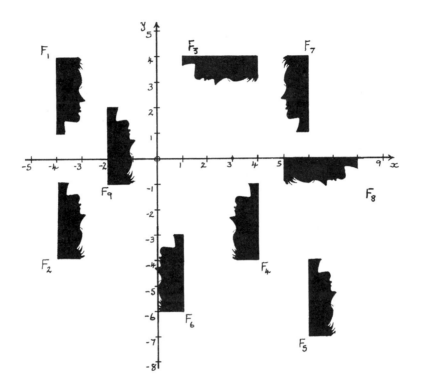

The diagram shows a face and its image under a variety of transformations. For example, F_5 is mapped (or transformed) onto F_7 by a rotation of $180°$ about the point $(6, -1.5)$. The position F_5 is referred to as the **object** and the new position F_7 as its **image**.

> (a) **Give examples, from the diagram, of a 90° rotation, a reflection and a translation.**
>
> (b) **What is the image of F_1 when it is rotated 180° about the origin?**

 TASKSHEET 1S - *Transformations*

Exercise 1

1. Describe fully in words the transformations which map:

    (a) F_1 to F_2 (b) F_2 to F_3

    (c) F_1 to F_4 (d) F_2 to F_5

    (e) F_3 to F_4 (f) F_1 to F_7

2. (a) F_2 is transformed to F_4 and then F_4 is transformed to F_3. Describe these two transformations. What single transformation maps F_2 to F_3 directly?

    (b) A reflection in $x = 1$ followed by a reflection in $y = 0$ is equivalent to a rotation about $(1, 0)$. Give an example of this using appropriate faces. What is the angle of rotation?

3. (a) F_8 is mapped onto F_5 by a rotation of $90°$ anti-clockwise about $(9, -3)$. The **inverse** of a transformation maps the image back onto the object. What is the inverse transformation in this case?

    (b) What is the inverse of a reflection?

4. (a) Applying any transformation and then its inverse is equivalent to the **identity** transformation. Describe the identity transformation.

    (b) What is the image of F_6 under the identity transformation?

24

2.2 Describing transformations

The point P (2, 1) is rotated 90° anticlockwise about the origin to give a new point, P', which has coordinates (−1, 2).

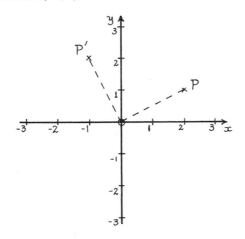

In general, it is easy to see that under a 90° anti-clockwise rotation about the origin (x, y) maps onto $(-y, x)$. In terms of position vectors, $\begin{bmatrix} x \\ y \end{bmatrix} \rightarrow \begin{bmatrix} -y \\ x \end{bmatrix}$.

This leads to a convenient way of describing the transformation by the matrix $\begin{bmatrix} 0 & -1 \\ 1 & 0 \end{bmatrix}$.

> **Verify that** $\begin{bmatrix} 0 & -1 \\ 1 & 0 \end{bmatrix}\begin{bmatrix} x \\ y \end{bmatrix} = \begin{bmatrix} -y \\ x \end{bmatrix}$

Express these transformations as mappings of $\begin{bmatrix} x \\ y \end{bmatrix}$ **and then write down matrices to represent them:**

(a) a reflection in the x axis;

(b) a half turn about the origin;

(c) a 90° clockwise rotation about the origin;

(d) an enlargement, scale factor 2, with centre at the origin.

$\begin{pmatrix} 2 \\ 1 \end{pmatrix} \rightarrow \begin{pmatrix} 2 \\ -1 \end{pmatrix}$ $\begin{pmatrix} x \\ y \end{pmatrix} \rightarrow \begin{pmatrix} x \\ -y \end{pmatrix}$

$\begin{bmatrix} 1 & 0 \\ 0 & -1 \end{bmatrix}\begin{bmatrix} x \\ y \end{bmatrix} = \begin{pmatrix} u \\ -y \end{pmatrix}$

$\times (x, y)$

$\times (x, -y)$

TASKSHEET 2 -Describing transformations

$\begin{pmatrix} 0 & 1 \\ -1 & 0 \end{pmatrix}$

2.3 Base vectors

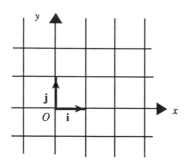

The two vectors **i** and **j**, of unit length, are called base vectors. They form two sides of a unit square in the first quadrant.

(a) Express i and j as column vectors.

(b) What are the images of i and j when the column vectors are multiplied by the matrices:

(i) $\begin{bmatrix} 1 & -1 \\ 1 & 1 \end{bmatrix}$ (ii) $\begin{bmatrix} 1 & 3 \\ -1 & 1 \end{bmatrix}$

(c) How are the image vectors related to the matrices?

In general, for a matrix $\begin{bmatrix} a & b \\ c & d \end{bmatrix}$, the images of the base vectors are:

$$\begin{bmatrix} a & b \\ c & d \end{bmatrix}\begin{bmatrix} 1 \\ 0 \end{bmatrix} = \begin{bmatrix} a \\ c \end{bmatrix} \qquad \begin{bmatrix} a & b \\ c & d \end{bmatrix}\begin{bmatrix} 0 \\ 1 \end{bmatrix} = \begin{bmatrix} b \\ d \end{bmatrix}$$

The two columns of a matrix give the images of the base vectors. This enables you to determine the matrix when it exists for any given transformation.

Example 1

Find the matrix for a half turn about the origin.

Solution

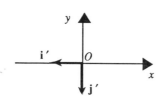

The diagram shows the images of the base vectors under a half turn about the origin.

$$\mathbf{i}' = \begin{bmatrix} -1 \\ 0 \end{bmatrix}, \quad \mathbf{j}' = \begin{bmatrix} 0 \\ -1 \end{bmatrix}$$

These form the columns of the matrix: $\begin{bmatrix} -1 & 0 \\ 0 & -1 \end{bmatrix}$

TASKSHEET 3 - *Base vectors*

26

The matrices for four of the transformations considered so far are given below:

1. **Two-way stretch with centre (0, 0), factor *a* in the *x* direction and factor *b* in the *y* direction.**

$$\begin{bmatrix} a & 0 \\ 0 & b \end{bmatrix}$$

2. **Shear**

   (i) *x*-axis invariant
   with $(0, 1) \rightarrow (k, 1)$ $\begin{bmatrix} 1 & k \\ 0 & 1 \end{bmatrix}$

   (ii) *y*-axis invariant
   with $(1, 0) \rightarrow (1, k)$ $\begin{bmatrix} 1 & 0 \\ k & 1 \end{bmatrix}$

3. **Rotation of angle θ anti-clockwise about (0, 0).** $\begin{bmatrix} \cos\theta & -\sin\theta \\ \sin\theta & \cos\theta \end{bmatrix}$

4. **Reflection in the line *y* = *x* tan θ** $\begin{bmatrix} \cos 2\theta & \sin 2\theta \\ \sin 2\theta & -\cos 2\theta \end{bmatrix}$

Example 2

What is the matrix for a reflection in the line $y = 1.5x$?

Solution

$\tan\theta = 1.5$

$\Rightarrow \theta = 56.3°$

$\Rightarrow 2\theta = 112.6°$

$\Rightarrow \cos 2\theta = -0.38$ and $\sin 2\theta = 0.92$, correct to 2 decimal places.

Required matrix $= \begin{bmatrix} -0.38 & 0.92 \\ 0.92 & 0.38 \end{bmatrix}$

> **Work out the matrices for:**
>
> (a) a 60° rotation about the origin;
>
> (b) a reflection in the line $y = 2x$.

2.4   Combining transformations

When referring to transformations and their associated matrices it is often convenient to use a notation involving a single letter.

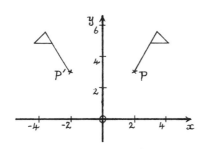

Point P on the flag is mapped onto its image P' by a reflection in the y-axis.

If this transformation is denoted by the single letter $\mathbf{Y}$, you can say:

$$\mathbf{Y}(P) = P'.$$

(a)   If P has position vector $\begin{bmatrix} 2 \\ 3 \end{bmatrix}$, what is its image P' where $P' = \mathbf{Y}(P)$?

(b)   What is the matrix for the transformation $\mathbf{Y}$?

(c)   How can the position vector of P' be obtained by a simple matrix multiplication?

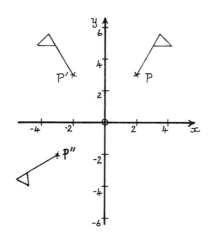

A quarter turn anti-clockwise about the origin is described by the matrix

$$\mathbf{Q} = \begin{bmatrix} 0 & -1 \\ 1 & 0 \end{bmatrix}$$

If this transformation is applied to the previous image P' to give a new image P'' then you can write $\mathbf{Q}(P') = P''$. Combining this equation with $P' = \mathbf{Y}(P)$ you can write:

$$\mathbf{Q}(\mathbf{Y}(P)) = P''$$

or,

$$\mathbf{QY}(P) = P''.$$

(a)   What single transformation is equivalent to $\mathbf{Y}$ followed by $\mathbf{Q}$?

(b)   What is the matrix for this equivalent transformation?

(c)   How is this matrix related to the matrices for $\mathbf{Y}$ and $\mathbf{Q}$?

(d)   With position vector $\begin{bmatrix} 2 \\ 3 \end{bmatrix}$ for P, find the position vector of P'' by matrix multiplication.

The matrix for a combined transformation is obtained by multiplying together the matrices of the respective transformations. In the example **QY** denoted transformation **Y** followed by transformation **Q**.

(a) **Why is it logical to let QY mean Y first, then Q, contrary to the order in which the expression is read?**

(b) **What does YQ mean?**

(c) **Find the image of *P* under YQ.**

(d) **Does YQ = QY?**

Note that the notation used for transformations is identical to that used for functions. You have seen, for example, that fg(*x*) means apply a function g first and then f. Geometric transformations are functions which operate on pairs of numbers (triples in 3 dimensions).

Exercise 2

1. **X** is a reflection in the *x*-axis; **Y** is a reflection in the *y*-axis.

    (a) What are the matrices **X, Y, XY, YX**?

    (b) Does **XY = YX**?

    (c) What single transformations are equivalent to **XY** and **YX**?

2. **M** is a reflection in the line *y* = *x*; **Q** is a quarter turn anti-clockwise about the origin.

    (a) What are the matrices **M, Q, MQ, QM**?

    (b) Does **MQ = QM**?

    (c) What single transformations are equivalent to **MQ** and **QM**?

3. Three shears are represented by matrices as follows:

$$S_1 = \begin{bmatrix} 1 & 1 \\ 0 & 1 \end{bmatrix} \qquad S_2 = \begin{bmatrix} 1 & -1 \\ 0 & 1 \end{bmatrix} \qquad S_3 = \begin{bmatrix} 1 & 0 \\ 1 & 1 \end{bmatrix}$$

    (a) Calculate $S_1 S_2$ and $S_2 S_1$ and comment on the result.

    (b) Calculate $S_1 S_3$ and $S_3 S_1$ and comment on the result.

TASKSHEET 4E - *Matrices and trigonometric identities*

2.5   Inverse transformations

A quarter turn anti-clockwise about the origin has been denoted by **Q**. The **inverse** transformation, which returns the image to the original position, is a quarter turn clockwise about the origin. This is denoted by $\mathbf{Q}^{-1}$. If $\mathbf{Q}(P) = P'$, then $\mathbf{Q}^{-1}(P') = P$.

For any transformation **T**, where $\mathbf{T}^{-1}$ denotes the inverse transformation:

$$\mathbf{T}^{-1}\mathbf{T} = \mathbf{T}\mathbf{T}^{-1} = \mathbf{I}.$$

Applying a transformation and then its inverse (or vice versa) is equivalent to leaving the object unchanged - the identity transformation.

With simple cases, reference to transformations enables an inverse matrix to be found. For example, **Q**, a quarter turn anti-clockwise about the origin, has inverse $\mathbf{Q}^{-1}$, which is a quarter turn clockwise about the origin.

You can immediately write down:

$$\mathbf{Q} = \begin{bmatrix} 0 & -1 \\ 1 & 0 \end{bmatrix} \quad \text{and} \quad \mathbf{Q}^{-1} = \begin{bmatrix} 0 & 1 \\ -1 & 0 \end{bmatrix}$$

and check that:

$$\mathbf{Q}^{-1}\mathbf{Q} = \begin{bmatrix} 0 & 1 \\ -1 & 0 \end{bmatrix}\begin{bmatrix} 0 & -1 \\ 1 & 0 \end{bmatrix} = \begin{bmatrix} 1 & 0 \\ 0 & 1 \end{bmatrix} = \mathbf{I}$$

Tasksheet 5 investigates how to find the inverse of a general matrix.

TASKSHEET 5 -*Inverse transformations*

The inverse of a matrix $\begin{bmatrix} a & b \\ c & d \end{bmatrix}$ is given by

$$\frac{1}{ad - bc} \begin{bmatrix} d & -b \\ -c & a \end{bmatrix}$$

where $ad - bc$ is the determinant of the matrix.

The determinant is the area scale factor for the transformation represented by the matrix. It is negative in the case of reflections or combined transformations which include an odd number of reflections.

Example 3

Calculate the inverse of $\mathbf{A} = \begin{bmatrix} 3 & 2 \\ -1 & 5 \end{bmatrix}$

Solution

The determinant of $\mathbf{A} = (3 \times 5) - (2 \times -1) = 17$

$$\Rightarrow \mathbf{A}^{-1} = \frac{1}{17}\begin{bmatrix} 5 & -2 \\ 1 & 3 \end{bmatrix}$$

Exercise 3

1. Find the determinants and inverses of these matrices

   (a) $\mathbf{A} = \begin{bmatrix} 3 & 4 \\ 2 & 5 \end{bmatrix}$ (b) $\mathbf{B} = \begin{bmatrix} 1 & -1 \\ 1 & 1 \end{bmatrix}$ (c) $\mathbf{C} = \begin{bmatrix} 2 & 1 \\ 2 & -3 \end{bmatrix}$

2. (a) Find the determinants of the matrices $\begin{bmatrix} 1 & -2 \\ 0 & 1 \end{bmatrix}$ and $\begin{bmatrix} 1 & 0 \\ 3 & 1 \end{bmatrix}$.

   (b) What kinds of transformation do these matrices represent?

   (c) What important property of these transformations is related to the value of the determinants?

   (d) Calculate the product of the two matrices in the order given in part (a). What do you expect the value of the determinant of the product to be?

   (e) Draw a diagram to show the image of the unit square under the transformation given by the product matrix.

   What is the area of the image?

2.6   Linear transformations

In considering the matrix representation of transformations a number of assumptions have been made. In particular, for transformations that can be represented by matrices, it has been assumed that:

(a)   the origin maps onto itself;

(b)   straight lines map onto straight lines;

(c)   pairs of parallel lines map onto pairs of parallel lines.

These assumptions are equivalent to the assumption that the standard square grid maps onto a grid of parallelograms with the origin unchanged.

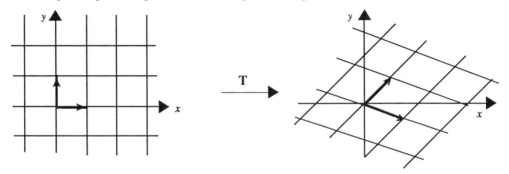

Transformations which satisfy these properties are known as **linear transformations**.

> (a)   **If a is the position vector of a general point, what can you say about the points λa, where λ is any real number?**
>
> (b)   **Show that T(λa) = λT(a) for a general matrix T.**
>
> (c)   **What is the significance of this result?**

   TASKSHEET 6 - *Linear transformations*

> **A linear transformation, T, satisfies the two properties:**
>
> (a)   **T (λa)   = λT(a)**
>
> (b) **T (a + b) = T (a) + T(b),**
>
> **for any vectors a and b and any real number λ.**

The fact that $T(x\mathbf{i} + y\mathbf{j}) = xT(\mathbf{i}) + yT(\mathbf{j})$ for any linear transformation T means that any point with position vector $\begin{bmatrix} x \\ y \end{bmatrix}$ referred to the usual square grid defined by $\mathbf{i}$ and $\mathbf{j}$ is mapped onto a corresponding point on a grid of parallelograms defined by $T(\mathbf{i})$ and $T(\mathbf{j})$.

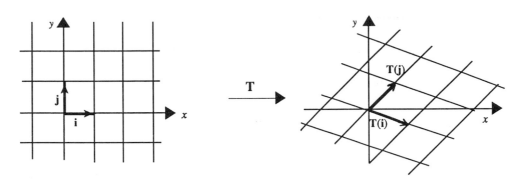

What happens to the square grid under the transformations given by these matrices?

(a) $A = \begin{bmatrix} 1 & 0 \\ 0 & 1 \end{bmatrix}$ (b) $B = \begin{bmatrix} 2 & -1 \\ -4 & 2 \end{bmatrix}$ (c) $C = \begin{bmatrix} 0 & 0 \\ 0 & 0 \end{bmatrix}$

It is important to note that not all transformations are linear, because not all transformations can be represented by matrices.

Which of the following transformations are linear and which are non-linear? In each case justify your answer.

(a)   Rotations about the origin.

(b)   Translations.

(c) $\begin{bmatrix} x \\ y \end{bmatrix} \rightarrow \begin{bmatrix} x^2 \\ y \end{bmatrix}$

(d) $\begin{bmatrix} x \\ y \end{bmatrix} \rightarrow \begin{bmatrix} x + y \\ x - y \end{bmatrix}$

After working through this chapter you should:

1. be able to determine the matrix, when it exists, for a given transformation and vice versa;

2. be familiar with the matrices of simple transformations;

3. be familiar with single letter notation for matrices and transformations;

4. understand how to combine transformations and find inverse transformations;

5. be familiar with the determinant of a 2 by 2 matrix and be able to find the inverse matrix, where possible;

6. understand linearity properties.

Transformations

1.

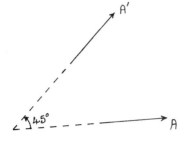

The arrow *A* has been rotated through 45° to *A'*.

Besides the angle, what **two** further pieces of information are required to fully describe a **rotation** ?

2. To describe a **reflection,** is it sufficient to give the position of the mirror line or is more information required?

3. A **translation** is usually described by a column vector, such as $\begin{bmatrix} 2 \\ -3 \end{bmatrix}$ meaning 2 units to the right and 3 units downward.

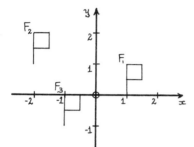

Describe the translations:

(a) F_1 to F_2

(b) F_2 to F_3

(c) F_3 to F_1

How does finding the sum of these three vectors act as a check on your answers?

4. An **enlargement** is described by giving the position of the centre of enlargement and the scale factor.

(a) If an object is enlarged by a scale factor of 2, what is the scale factor of the 'enlargement', with the same centre, which returns the image to the original position? Why is 'enlargement' printed in inverted commas?

(b) What transformation is equivalent to an enlargement with a scale factor of –1?

(c) Explain carefully, with the aid of a diagram, the effect of enlarging with a scale factor of –2.

5. The **identity** transformation leaves an object unchanged in shape, size and position. A rotation through 360°, either clockwise or anti-clockwise, about any centre, is equivalent to the identity. Describe the identity in terms of:

(a) a translation

(b) an enlargement.

(continued)

35

6.   The **inverse** of a transformation returns the image to its original position. What is the inverse of:

(a)   a translation $\begin{bmatrix} -6 \\ 11 \end{bmatrix}$

(b)   a clockwise rotation of 120° about (3, –4)

(c)   an enlargement with scale factor $-\frac{1}{2}$, centre (0,0)

(d)   a reflection in $y = \frac{1}{2}x$.

7.

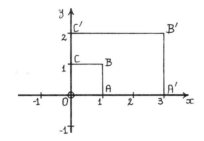

The square *OABC* in the diagram has been given a **two-way stretch**, with factors 3 and 2 in the *x* and *y* directions, to give the image rectangle *OA'B'C'*.

On a copy of the diagram draw the image of *OABC* after two way stretches with factors:

(a)   2 and 1   (b)   –2 and 2   (c)   3 and –1

8.

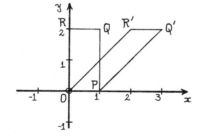

The rectangle *OPQR* has been given a **shear** which has mapped it onto the parallelogram *OPQ'R'*.

A shear is described by giving the invariant line (the *x*-axis here) and the image of a point not on that line (for example, (1, 1) → (2, 1)).

Draw diagrams to show the image of *OPQR* under shears with:

(a)   invariant line : $y = 0$ (1, 1) → (–1, 1)

(b)   invariant line : $x = 0$ (1, 0) → (1, –1)

Describing transformations

1.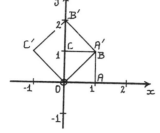

   The 'unit square' $OABC$ has been mapped onto the square $OA'B'C'$ by a transformation which involves both a rotation and an enlargement.

   (a) Describe in detail the rotation and enlargement.
   Does it matter which transformation is done first?

   (b) Write down the position vectors of the vertices O, A, B and C and their images, the vertices O, A', B' and C'.

   (c) Write down the images of the following points on the line AB :

   $$\begin{bmatrix} 1 \\ 0 \end{bmatrix} \quad \begin{bmatrix} 1 \\ 0.2 \end{bmatrix} \quad \begin{bmatrix} 1 \\ 0.4 \end{bmatrix} \quad \begin{bmatrix} 1 \\ 0.6 \end{bmatrix} \quad \begin{bmatrix} 1 \\ 0.8 \end{bmatrix} \quad \begin{bmatrix} 1 \\ 1 \end{bmatrix}$$

   (d) Suggest possible values for a, b, c, d if the transformation is described by:

   $$\begin{bmatrix} x \\ y \end{bmatrix} \rightarrow \begin{bmatrix} ax + by \\ cx + dy \end{bmatrix}$$

   (e) What is the matrix for the transformation?
   Check that your suggestion gives correct results for other points on the figure.

2.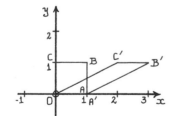

   This 'unit square' $OABC$ has been mapped onto the parallelogram $OAB'C'$ by a transformation which is known as a **shear**.

   (a) Describe the main features of this transformation.

   (b) Write down the images under the shear of the set of points given in part (c) of question 1.

   (c) What is the matrix for this transformation?

   (continued)

3.

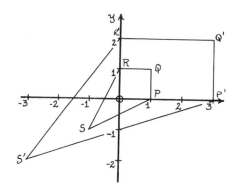

A quadrilateral *PQRS* has been mapped onto another quadrilateral *P'Q'R'S'* by a transformation known as a **two-way stretch**.

(a) Describe the main features of this two-way stretch.

(b) How does a two-way stretch differ from an enlargement?

(c) Write down the coordinates of the points *P*, *Q*, *R* and *S* and their images *P'*, *Q'*, *R'* and *S'*.

(d) What is the matrix for this transformation?

4.

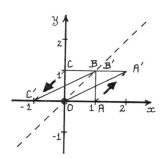

A unit square *OABC* is mapped onto a parallelogram *OA'BC'*. As in question 2, the transformation involved is a **shear**. The points *O* and *B* remain fixed and lie on the **invariant line** of the shear. Other points move parallel to this line, in opposite directions on either side, as indicated by the arrows in the diagram above.

(a) Write down the images under this shear of the set of points on *AB* given in part (c) of question 1 .

(b) Suggest possible values for *a*, *b*, *c*, *d* if the transformation is described by:

$$\begin{bmatrix} x \\ y \end{bmatrix} \rightarrow \begin{bmatrix} ax + by \\ cx + dy \end{bmatrix}$$

(c) Suggest a matrix for this shear and check that it works for other points on the figure.

Base vectors

$$\begin{bmatrix} a & b \\ c & d \end{bmatrix}\begin{bmatrix} 1 \\ 0 \end{bmatrix} = \begin{bmatrix} a \\ c \end{bmatrix} \qquad \begin{bmatrix} a & b \\ c & d \end{bmatrix}\begin{bmatrix} 0 \\ 1 \end{bmatrix} = \begin{bmatrix} b \\ d \end{bmatrix}$$

$ps\ (1,0)$
$\quad (0,1)$

1.   For the following transformations draw a diagram to show the effect on the base
      vectors **i** and **j.** Then write down the matrix for the transformation.

   (a)   A reflection in the x -axis.

   (b)   The identity transformation.

   (c)   A half turn about the origin.

   (d)   A reflection in $y = -x$.

   (e)   An enlargement scale factor 2, centre $(0, 0)$

   (f)   A quarter turn clockwise about $(0, 0)$.

   (g)   A two-way stretch in the x and y directions with factors 2 and 1.5.

   (h)   A shear with x-axis invariant and $(0, 1) \rightarrow (1, 1)$

2.   For each of the following matrices draw a diagram to show their effect on the base
      vectors and then describe the transformations which they represent.

   (a) $\begin{bmatrix} 0 & -1 \\ 1 & 0 \end{bmatrix}$ (b) $\begin{bmatrix} 1 & -1 \\ 0 & 1 \end{bmatrix}$ (c) $\begin{bmatrix} 0.5 & 0 \\ 0 & 0.5 \end{bmatrix}$ (d) $\begin{bmatrix} 0 & 1 \\ 1 & 0 \end{bmatrix}$

   (e) $\begin{bmatrix} 2 & 0 \\ 0 & 1 \end{bmatrix}$ (f) $\begin{bmatrix} -1 & 0 \\ 0 & 1 \end{bmatrix}$

(continued)

3. The diagram shows the two base vectors after a rotation through an angle θ about the origin.

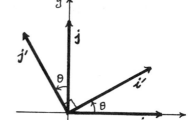

(a) Explain why $\begin{bmatrix} 1 \\ 0 \end{bmatrix} \rightarrow \begin{bmatrix} \cos\theta \\ \sin\theta \end{bmatrix}$.

(b) What is the image of $\begin{bmatrix} 0 \\ 1 \end{bmatrix}$?

(c) Write down the matrix for a rotation of angle θ about the origin.

(d) Write down, using your result, the matrices for rotations though angles of 0°, 90°, 180°, 270° about the origin. Compare your answers with those obtained in question 1.

4.

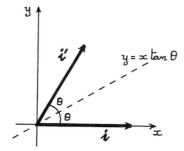

The diagram shows the image of *i* on reflection in the line $y = x \tan\theta$ (a line throught the origin making an angle θ with the *x*-axis).

(a) Find the images of $\begin{bmatrix} 1 \\ 0 \end{bmatrix}$ and $\begin{bmatrix} 0 \\ 1 \end{bmatrix}$.

(b) Write down the matrix for a reflection in $y = x \tan\theta$.

(c) Check that your result agrees with the matrices for the reflections in question 1.

Matrices and trigonometric identities

1.   Two anti-clockwise rotations through angles θ and ϕ about the origin are denoted by $\mathbf{R}_\theta$, $\mathbf{R}_\phi$

(a)   Explain why $\mathbf{R}_\theta \mathbf{R}_\phi = \mathbf{R}_\phi \mathbf{R}_\theta$.

(b)   Write down the matrices $\mathbf{R}_\theta$ and $\mathbf{R}_\phi$ and then calculate the matrix $\mathbf{R}_\theta \mathbf{R}_\phi$.

(c)   What single transformation does $\mathbf{R}_\theta \mathbf{R}_\phi$ represent?

(d)   How do your results demonstrate that:

$$\cos(\theta + \phi) = \cos\theta\cos\phi - \sin\theta\sin\phi\ ?$$

(e)   What is the corresponding result for $\sin(\theta + \phi)$?

2.   A rotation through an angle θ about the origin is considered by convention to be anti-clockwise. The corresponding clockwise rotation would then be denoted by $\mathbf{R}_{-\theta}$.

(a)   Explain why $\mathbf{R}_{-\theta}\mathbf{R}_\theta = \mathbf{I}$, where $\mathbf{I}$ is the identity transformation.

(b)   Explain, using the graphs of $\sin\theta$ and $\cos\theta$, why $\cos(-\theta) = \cos\theta$ and $\sin(-\theta) = -\sin\theta$.

(c)   Write down the matrix for $\mathbf{R}_{-\theta}$ in its simplest form using the results of part (b).

(d)   Calculate $\mathbf{R}_{-\theta}\mathbf{R}_\theta$ and use your result to show that $\cos^2\theta + \sin^2\theta = 1$.

3.   A reflection in the line $y = x\tan\theta$ is denoted by $\mathbf{M}_\theta$.

(a)   Write down the matrix.

(b)   Calculate $\mathbf{M}_\theta^2$ and comment on the result.

Inverse transformations

1. A transformation **M** has matrix $\begin{bmatrix} 4 & 1 \\ 3 & 2 \end{bmatrix}$.

   You can use the fact that $\mathbf{M}^{-1}\,\mathbf{M} = \mathbf{I}$ to find the inverse matrix $\mathbf{M}^{-1}$.

   Let $\mathbf{M}^{-1} = \begin{bmatrix} p & q \\ r & s \end{bmatrix}$, where p, q, r, s are numbers to be found.

   Then, $\mathbf{M}^{-1}\,\mathbf{M} = \begin{bmatrix} p & q \\ r & s \end{bmatrix}\begin{bmatrix} 4 & 1 \\ 3 & 2 \end{bmatrix} = \begin{bmatrix} 1 & 0 \\ 0 & 1 \end{bmatrix}$

   (a) Show that $4p + 3q = 1$
   $$p + 2q = 0$$

   (b) Solve this pair of simultaneous equations.

   (c) Find two other simultaneous equations involving r and s. Solve these equations.

   (d) Show from this that $\mathbf{M}^{-1} = \dfrac{1}{5}\begin{bmatrix} 2 & -1 \\ -3 & 4 \end{bmatrix}$

   (e) Check that $\mathbf{M}^{-1}\,\mathbf{M} = \mathbf{I}$

   (f) Let P be a point with position vector $\begin{bmatrix} -2 \\ 5 \end{bmatrix}$

   Calculate $P' = \mathbf{M}(P)$. Check that $\mathbf{M}^{-1}(P') = P$

2. Use a similar procedure to find the inverse of the matrix $\begin{bmatrix} 5 & -1 \\ -2 & 2 \end{bmatrix}$.

3. Using the same procedure for the matrix $\mathbf{M} = \begin{bmatrix} a & b \\ c & d \end{bmatrix}$, you can produce a general result for $\mathbf{M}^{-1}$.

   $$\mathbf{M}^{-1}\,\mathbf{M} = \begin{bmatrix} p & q \\ r & s \end{bmatrix}\begin{bmatrix} a & b \\ c & d \end{bmatrix} = \begin{bmatrix} 1 & 0 \\ 0 & 1 \end{bmatrix}$$

   (a) Explain why: $ap + cq = 1$
   $$bp + dq = 0$$

   (b) Solve these simultaneous equations to give
   $$p = \frac{d}{ad - bc}\,, \quad q = \frac{-b}{ad - bc}$$

   (c) Find two simultaneous equations involving r and s and solve them.

   (d) Show that $\mathbf{M}^{-1} = \dfrac{1}{ad - bc}\begin{bmatrix} d & -b \\ -c & a \end{bmatrix}$

   (continued)

(e)   Check that this agrees with the results of questions 1 and 2.

(f)   Use the result to find the inverse of $\begin{bmatrix} 2 & -5 \\ 1 & 2 \end{bmatrix}$

4.   The expression $ad - bc$ is known as the **determinant** of the matrix and it has a number of important properties.

The matrix $\begin{bmatrix} a & b \\ c & d \end{bmatrix}$ maps the unit square onto a parallelogram as shown.

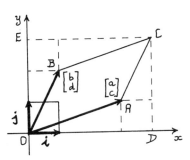

(a)   What is the position vector of C ?

(b)   What is the area of rectangle $ODCE$ in terms of a, b, c and d ?

(c)   What are the areas of the two small rectangles and the four triangles surrounding the parallelogram $OACB$?

(d)   Show that the area of the parallelogram is equal to the determinant $ad - bc$.

5.   (a)   What transformations do the following matrices represent ?

(i) $\begin{bmatrix} 2 & 0 \\ 0 & 2 \end{bmatrix}$ (ii) $\begin{bmatrix} 1 & 2 \\ 0 & 1 \end{bmatrix}$ (iii) $\begin{bmatrix} 0 & 1 \\ -1 & 0 \end{bmatrix}$ (iv) $\begin{bmatrix} 2 & 0 \\ 0 & 3 \end{bmatrix}$

(b)   Draw diagrams to show the image of the unit square for each.

(c)   Calculate the determinant in each case and comment on your findings.

6.   (a)   Find the determinant for the following reflections:

(i) $\begin{bmatrix} -1 & 0 \\ 0 & 1 \end{bmatrix}$ (ii) $\begin{bmatrix} 0 & 1 \\ 1 & 0 \end{bmatrix}$ (iii) $\begin{bmatrix} 0 & -1 \\ -1 & 0 \end{bmatrix}$ (iv) $\begin{bmatrix} 0.8 & 0.6 \\ 0.6 & -0.8 \end{bmatrix}$

(b)   Comment on the results.

Linear transformations

1. Find the images of the following points on the line $y = \frac{3}{2}x$

$$\begin{bmatrix} 2 \\ 3 \end{bmatrix} \quad \begin{bmatrix} 4 \\ 6 \end{bmatrix} \quad \begin{bmatrix} 6 \\ 9 \end{bmatrix} \quad \begin{bmatrix} 0 \\ 0 \end{bmatrix} \quad \begin{bmatrix} -2 \\ -3 \end{bmatrix} \quad \begin{bmatrix} -4 \\ -6 \end{bmatrix}$$

under the transformations represented by:

(a) $\begin{bmatrix} 2 & -1 \\ 1 & 2 \end{bmatrix}$ (b) $\begin{bmatrix} 1 & 3 \\ 0 & 1 \end{bmatrix}$

What do you notice about the two sets of image vectors?

2. (a) Calculate: (i) $\begin{bmatrix} p & q \\ r & s \end{bmatrix}\begin{bmatrix} x \\ y \end{bmatrix}$ (ii) $\begin{bmatrix} p & q \\ r & s \end{bmatrix}\begin{bmatrix} \lambda x \\ \lambda y \end{bmatrix}$

(b) How do your results show that $\mathbf{T}(\lambda\mathbf{a}) = \lambda\mathbf{T}(\mathbf{a})$,

where $\mathbf{T} = \begin{bmatrix} p & q \\ r & s \end{bmatrix}$ and $\mathbf{a} = \begin{bmatrix} x \\ y \end{bmatrix}$?

(c) What general statement can you make about the image of a straight line through the origin under a transformation $\mathbf{T}$?

(d) What is the image of the origin under a transformation $\mathbf{T}$?

3. (a) Calculate: (i) $\begin{bmatrix} p & q \\ r & s \end{bmatrix}\begin{bmatrix} x_1 \\ y_1 \end{bmatrix}$ (ii) $\begin{bmatrix} p & q \\ r & s \end{bmatrix}\begin{bmatrix} x_2 \\ y_2 \end{bmatrix}$ (iii) $\begin{bmatrix} p & q \\ r & s \end{bmatrix}\begin{bmatrix} x_1 + x_2 \\ y_1 + y_2 \end{bmatrix}$

(b) How do these results show that $\mathbf{T}(\mathbf{a} + \mathbf{b}) = \mathbf{T}(\mathbf{a}) + \mathbf{T}(\mathbf{b})$, where

$$\mathbf{T} = \begin{bmatrix} p & q \\ r & s \end{bmatrix}, \quad \mathbf{a} = \begin{bmatrix} x_1 \\ y_1 \end{bmatrix} \text{ and } \mathbf{b} = \begin{bmatrix} x_2 \\ y_2 \end{bmatrix} ?$$

(continued)

4.

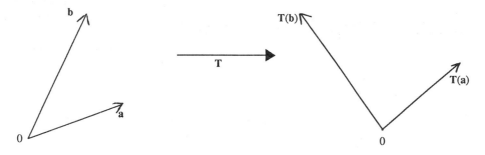

a and **b** are two vectors which map onto the vectors **T(a)** and **T(b)**. Copy the two diagrams and mark the vector **a + b** on the first and the vector **T(a) + T(b)** on the second. What is the significance of the result that

$$T(a + b) \; = \; T(a) + T(b)$$

in terms of the diagrams you have drawn?

> **A linear transformation, T, satisfies the two properties**
>
> (a) $\qquad T(\lambda a) \; = \; \lambda T(a)$
>
> (b) $\qquad T(a + b) \; = \; T(a) + T(b)$
>
> **where a and b are two vectors and λ is any real number.**

5. The position vector $\mathbf{r} \; = \begin{bmatrix} 5 \\ 3 \end{bmatrix}$ can be written in the form

$$\mathbf{r} = 5\begin{bmatrix} 1 \\ 0 \end{bmatrix} + 3\begin{bmatrix} 0 \\ 1 \end{bmatrix} = 5\mathbf{i} + 3\mathbf{j} \, ,$$

where **i** and **j** represent the two base vectors $\begin{bmatrix} 1 \\ 0 \end{bmatrix}$ and $\begin{bmatrix} 0 \\ 1 \end{bmatrix}$.

Find the images **T(i)** and **T(j)** of the base vectors **i** and **j** and **T(r)**, the image of **r**, for the following matrices. Verify in each case that:

$$T(5\mathbf{i} + 3\mathbf{j}) \; = \; 5T(\mathbf{i}) + 3T(\mathbf{j})$$

(a) $\quad T = \begin{bmatrix} 3 & 2 \\ 1 & 1 \end{bmatrix}$ (b) $\quad T = \begin{bmatrix} 1 & 1 \\ -1 & 1 \end{bmatrix}$ (c) $\quad T = \begin{bmatrix} 2 & 5 \\ 0 & -3 \end{bmatrix}$

6. Suppose **i** and **j** define the usual square grid and **T(i)** and **T(j)** define a grid of parallelograms with the origin unchanged.

Show that $\mathbf{T}\,(x\mathbf{i} + y\mathbf{j}) \; = \; x\mathbf{T}\,(\mathbf{i}) + yT(\mathbf{j})$, using the two linearity properties. What is the significance of this result?

Tutorial sheet

1. $\mathbf{A} = \begin{bmatrix} 0 & 1 \\ 1 & 0 \end{bmatrix}$ and $\mathbf{B} = \begin{bmatrix} 0 & -1 \\ 1 & 0 \end{bmatrix}$

    (a) Describe fully the transformations represented by the matrices **A** and **B**.

    (b) Calculate the matrix products **AB** and **BA**.

    (c) Describe fully the transformations represented by the matrices **AB** and **BA**.

    (d) Write down the determinants of the matrices **A** and **B** and comment on their significance.

    (e) Find the inverse matrices $\mathbf{A}^{-1}$ and $\mathbf{B}^{-1}$ and describe the transformations that they represent.

2. Write down matrices for each of the following transformations:

    (a) a two-way stretch with centre at the origin with scale factors 2 in the x direction and 2.5 in the y direction;

    (b) a shear with the y-axis invariant, such that the point $(1, 0)$ maps onto $(1, -2)$;

    (c) a rotation of $120°$ anti-clockwise about the origin;

    (d) a reflection in the line $y = 0.5x$.

3. In each case in question 2, describe the inverse transformation and write down the corresponding matrix.

4. Find the determinants and inverses of the following matrices:

    (a) $\begin{bmatrix} 2 & 1 \\ 1 & 2 \end{bmatrix}$ (b) $\begin{bmatrix} 3 & -2 \\ -2 & 1 \end{bmatrix}$ (c) $\begin{bmatrix} 0.6 & -0.8 \\ 0.8 & 0.6 \end{bmatrix}$ (d) $\begin{bmatrix} 0.6 & -0.8 \\ -0.8 & -0.6 \end{bmatrix}$

5. What are the two main properties of a **linear** transformation?

(continued)

6.   Which of the following transformations are **linear** and which are **non-linear** ?

(a)   Enlargement, centre $(0, 0)$, scale factor 2.

(b)   Rotation of $75°$ clockwise about $(1, 0)$.

(c)   Translation: $\begin{bmatrix} x \\ y \end{bmatrix} \rightarrow \begin{bmatrix} x \\ y \end{bmatrix} + \begin{bmatrix} 4 \\ -1 \end{bmatrix}$

(d)   Reflection in $y = 2x$.

7.   Explain carefully why translations are not **linear** transformations.

8.   Transformations in 3 dimensions can often be represented by 3 x 3 matrices.

Consider

$$\mathbf{A} = \begin{bmatrix} 0 & 0 & 1 \\ 0 & 1 & 0 \\ 1 & 0 & 0 \end{bmatrix} \text{ and } \mathbf{B} = \begin{bmatrix} 0 & 0 & -1 \\ 0 & 1 & 0 \\ -1 & 0 & 0 \end{bmatrix}$$

(a)   Describe fully the transformations represented by the matrices **A** and **B**.

(b)   Calculate the matrix products **AB** and **BA**.

(c)   Describe fully the transformations represented by the matrices **AB** and **BA**.

3 Simultaneous equations

3.1 Introduction

The problem of finding where two straight lines cross is the same as the problem of finding values for x and y which simultaneously satisfy two equations.

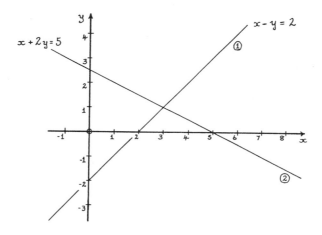

You can solve equations geometrically, by drawing the graphs and finding their point of intersection. However, it is usually much quicker to use an algebraic method.

> **Give an algebraic solution of**
>
> $x + 2y = 5$ ①
>
> $x - y = 2$ ②

Extra practice of algebraic methods is given on Tasksheet 1S

 TASKSHEET 1S - *Elimination*

2 equations in 2 unknowns such as those in the example above are often referred to as **2 x 2 simultaneous equations**. There is a straightforward connection with 2 x 2 matrices because the two equations can be written as the matrix equation:

$$\begin{bmatrix} 1 & 2 \\ 1 & -1 \end{bmatrix} \begin{bmatrix} x \\ y \end{bmatrix} = \begin{bmatrix} 5 \\ 2 \end{bmatrix}.$$

This leads to an alternative method of solving simultaneous equations which is introduced in the discussion point.

(a) **What point is transformed by the matrix $\begin{bmatrix} 1 & 2 \\ 1 & -1 \end{bmatrix}$ into the point (5, 2)?**

(b) **What alternative method of solving simultaneous equations is suggested by your answer to (a)?**

(c) **What are the practical advantages and disadvantages of the methods available for solving a pair of simultaneous equations?**

In the following example, simultaneous equations are solved using the inverse matrix. In practice, matrix format is often used for equations although it is usually best to use an elimination method for the actual solution. Whatever method is used, clearly laid out solutions are essential.

Example 1

Find the point of intersection of the two lines

$$2x + 3y = 5 \qquad ①$$
$$3x - 4y = -1 \qquad ②$$

Solution

$$\begin{bmatrix} 2 & 3 \\ 3 & -4 \end{bmatrix} \begin{bmatrix} x \\ y \end{bmatrix} = \begin{bmatrix} 5 \\ -1 \end{bmatrix} \Rightarrow \begin{bmatrix} x \\ y \end{bmatrix} = \frac{1}{-17} \begin{bmatrix} -4 & -3 \\ -3 & 2 \end{bmatrix} \begin{bmatrix} 5 \\ -1 \end{bmatrix}$$

$$\Rightarrow \begin{bmatrix} x \\ y \end{bmatrix} = -\frac{1}{17} \begin{bmatrix} -17 \\ -17 \end{bmatrix} = \begin{bmatrix} 1 \\ 1 \end{bmatrix}$$

The lines intersect at the point (1, 1).

Exercise 1

1. The point C is transformed by the matrix $\begin{bmatrix} 1 & -4 \\ 2 & 1 \end{bmatrix}$ to the point $C'(6, 3)$. What are the coordinates of C ?

2. The lines

$$2x - y = a$$
$$x + 4y = b$$

intersect at (3, –2). What are the values of a and b ?

3. Find the coordinates of D, the point of intersection of the lines

$$y = x + 5$$
$$2y = 5 - 3x$$

3.2   Geometrical ideas

Some problems can give rise to unexpected complications. When difficulties arise, a geometrical understanding can prove advantageous.

For any value of a, consider the simultaneous equations

$$2x + 3y = 5$$

$$2x + 3y = a$$

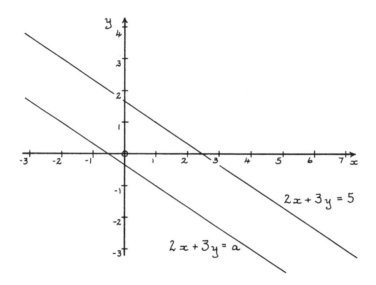

> (a)   **What difficulty arises when solving these equations with algebraic methods?**
>
> (b)   **What geometrical property do you notice?**
>
> (c)   **Describe what happens as a varies.**

You have seen that 2 x 2 simultaneous equations have either:

(i)   no solution

or

(ii)   a unique solution

or

(iii)   infinitely many solutions.

Exercise 2

1. Using geometry, explain why the following simultaneous equations have no solution.

    $$s + 2t = 3$$

    $$4t = 5 - 2s$$

2. Construct pairs of simultaneous equations of the form

    $$a_1 x + b_1 y = c_1$$

    $$a_2 x + b_2 y = c_2$$

    so that

    (a)   the solution set has a unique element;

    (b)   there are no solutions;

    (c)   the solution set has an infinite number of elements.

3. For the lines with equations

    $$ax + 3y = 4$$

    $$x - by = 2$$

    (a)   state values of a and b for which there is no solution;

    (b)   state values of a and b for which there are infinitely many solutions;

    (c)   show that
    $$x = \frac{2(3 + 2b)}{(ab + 3)}$$
    and
    $$y = \frac{2(2 - a)}{(ab + 3)}$$

    (d)   give conditions for the lines to be parallel.

3.3 Crushing transformations

Solving simultaneous equations by matrix methods is equivalent to the geometric problem of finding a point which is transformed to an image point. One method of solution is therefore to apply the inverse transformation from the image back to the original point. Algebraically this means using the inverse matrix.

You have seen that the simultaneous equations

$$2x + 3y = 5 \quad \text{or} \quad \begin{bmatrix} 2 & 3 \\ 2 & 3 \end{bmatrix} \begin{bmatrix} x \\ y \end{bmatrix} = \begin{bmatrix} 5 \\ a \end{bmatrix}$$

lead to non-unique solutions.

To discover what is happening geometrically, you need to investigate the nature of the transformation.

TASKSHEET 2 - *Destroying a dimension*

The transformation $\begin{bmatrix} 2 & 3 \\ 2 & 3 \end{bmatrix}$ crushes all the points in the (x, y) plane onto a line. Note that the determinant or area scale factor is 0.

> **A matrix M represents a crushing transformation if $|M| = 0$.**

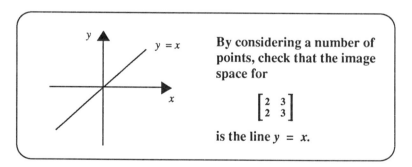

By considering a number of points, check that the image space for

$$\begin{bmatrix} 2 & 3 \\ 2 & 3 \end{bmatrix}$$

is the line $y = x$.

If $a = 5$ then $(5, a)$ is a possible image since it is on the line $y = x$ and the equations are **consistent**. Consistency means that the equations can be solved. In this case, solutions lie on the line which is crushed onto $(5, 5)$ by the transformation.

> **Check that the image of any point on the line $3y = 5 - 2x$ is $(5, 5)$.**

If $a \neq 5$ then $(5, a)$ does not lie on the line $y = x$ and so no points can be found which transform to $(5, a)$. The equations are then **inconsistent** and equality cannot be true for both equations simultaneously.

3.4 Elimination

So far only 2 x 2 simultaneous equations have been studied, but for practical applications the number of unknowns and equations can be much greater.

Consider the set of simultaneous equations

$$2x - y = 3 \qquad ①$$

$$x + 4y = 6 \qquad ②$$

$$3x - 5y = a \qquad ③$$

$$2② - ①, \quad 9y = 9$$

$$\Rightarrow \quad y = 1$$

In ②, $\qquad x = 2$

> **Explain how the solution set depends upon the value of *a*.**

When this 3 x 2 set of simultaneous equations have a solution they are said to be **consistent**. This means the solution for the first two equations is also the solution for the "extra" third equation.

Consider the set of simultaneous equations

$$2x - y - z = 6 \qquad ①$$
$$3x + y - 4z = -1 \qquad ②$$

$$① + ②, \quad 5x - 5z = 5$$

$$\Rightarrow \quad x = 1 + z$$

$$3① - 2②, \quad -5y + 5z = 20$$

$$y = -4 + z$$

> (a) **Why is the solution not unique ?**
>
> (b) **How would a third equation affect the situation ?**

> **Simultaneous equations only have a unique solution
> if there are at least as many equations as variables.**

Early on in this chapter, you were asked which method you would choose to solve simultaneous equations. The method of elimination can be applied to large systems and used repeatedly until the value of one variable is found.

Example 2

Solve

$$2x - y + 4z = 11 \qquad ①$$

$$x + 3y - 3z = -3 \qquad ②$$

$$x - 2y + z = 6 \qquad ③$$

Solution

$$① - 2②, \quad -7y + 10z = 17 \quad ④$$

$$② - ③, \qquad 5y - 4z = -9 \quad ⑤$$

> **Why choose to eliminate x first?**

$$2④ + 5⑤, \qquad 11y = -11$$

$$\Rightarrow \quad y = -1$$

in ④,

$$10z = 10$$

$$\Rightarrow \quad z = 1$$

in ③,

$$x = 6 - 2 - 1$$

$$\Rightarrow \quad x = 3$$

The solution is $x = 3$, $y = -1$ and $z = 1$.

The above example shows that the method of elimination extends to larger systems, although care and organisation in presenting your solutions are important. However, in the 2 x 2 case, you have seen that problems occur with this method and so a general method which deals with these difficulties may be needed. It is often best to assume that a unique solution exists and go ahead on that premise. If things go wrong, then it may be necessary to bring a powerful general method into action.

Exercise 3

1. Solve

$$x - 3y + z = -2$$

$$2x + 2y - z = 7$$

$$x - 5y + 3z = -6$$

2. Solve

$$7x - y + 4z = 4$$

$$2x + 5y - 3z = 23$$

$$6x - 2y + 5z = -4$$

3. Solve the set of simultaneous equations with 4 unknowns

$$x + y + z + t = 3$$

$$-x + y - z + 2t = 5$$

$$x - 3y + z - t = -5$$

$$4x + y - 2z + t = 9$$

4. The following set of simultaneous equations have a unique solution

$$2x - y + 7z = 5$$

$$3x + 4y + 2z = 2$$

$$5x - 3y + 2z = 13$$

$$3x - 2y + z = a$$

   (a) What is the unique solution?

   (b) What is the value of a ?

3.5 Planes

It is both instructive and interesting to study in more detail the case of 3 x 3 simultaneous equations and a geometric interpretation. Just as the equation of a line has the form $ax + by = c$ the equation of a plane has the form $ax + by + cz = d$.

In the picture, the two sloping planes which form the roof intersect to form a line, the ridge of the roof. The front and rear wall of the building are parallel and do not intersect.

> **How many different configurations of three planes can you find ?**

The solution sets for the intersection of three non-parallel planes can be categorised by one of the following cases.

A   Unique solution, the planes intersect at a point.

B   Infinitely many solutions, the planes form a sheaf.

C   No solution, the planes form a hollow prism.

A.   B.   C.

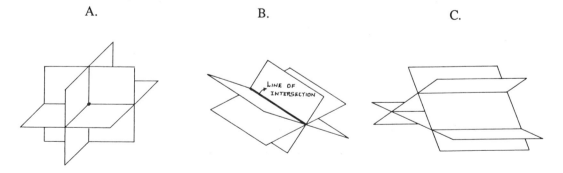

> **How can you recognise when planes are parallel from their equations ?**

Example 3

For each of the cases (a) $a = -1, b = 2$, (b) $a = 5, b = -16$, (c) $a = 5, b = 3$, solve the set of simultaneous equations

$$2x - y - z = 6 \qquad ①$$
$$3x + y - 4z = -1 \qquad ②$$
$$4x + ay - 9z = b \qquad ③$$

In each case describe the solution geometrically.

Solution

It is easy to see by inspection that no two planes are parallel, so geometrically the solution must represent a point, a sheaf or a prism

Equations ① and ② do not involve a and b.

$$① + ②, \quad 5x \quad - 5z = 5$$

$$\Rightarrow x \quad -z = 1 \quad ④$$

$$3① - 2②, \quad -5y + 5z = 20$$

$$\Rightarrow \quad -y + z = 4 \quad ⑤$$

Equations ④ and ⑤ can be used to eliminate x and y from equation ③ :

$$③ - 4④ + a⑤, \quad (a-5)z = 4a + b - 4 \quad ⑥$$

(a)　In ⑥ , putting $a = -1, b = 2, -6z = -6 \Rightarrow z = 1$

　　In ④ and ⑤ , $x = 2, y = -3, z = 1$.

　　The 3 planes intersect at a single point.

(b)　In ⑥ , putting $a = 5, b = -16, \ 0z = 0$ gives no restriction on z.

　　The equations have infinitely many solutions. If z is assigned the arbitrary value λ,

$$x = 1 + \lambda, \ y = -4 + \lambda, \ z = \lambda \ \text{ for any } \lambda.$$

　　The three planes form a sheaf.

(c)　In ⑥ , putting $a = 5, b = 3, \ 0z = 19$

　　The equations are inconsistent. The planes form a prism.

Exercise 4

1. Find the point of intersection of the three planes

    $$3x - y + 4z = 4$$
    $$2x + 3y - 2z = -15$$
    $$2x - 4y + z = 1$$

2. Find the equation of the line of intersection of the three planes

    $$2x - 5y + 3z = 3$$
    $$3x + 2y - 5z = -5$$
    $$5x - 22y + 17z = 17$$

3. Show, algebraically, that the following three planes form a prism.

    $$x + y - z = 0$$
    $$3x - 4y - z = 9$$
    $$5x - 2y - 3z = 15$$

4. Find the solutions of the simultaneous equations

    $$7x - 3y + z = 19$$
    $$2x - 5y + z = b$$
    $$x + ay - 2z = 19$$

    when

    (a) $a = 3$, $b = -3$ (b) $a = 12$, $b = 0$ (c) $a = 12$, $b = 7$

    In each case describe the solution geometrically.

After working through this chapter you should:

1. know that 2×2 simultaneous linear equations can be written as

$$\begin{bmatrix} a_1 & b_1 \\ a_2 & b_2 \end{bmatrix} \begin{bmatrix} x \\ y \end{bmatrix} = \begin{bmatrix} c_1 \\ c_2 \end{bmatrix}$$

2. understand that the solution of two simultaneous linear equations

$$a_1 x + b_1 y = c_1$$

$$a_2 x + b_2 y = c_2$$

can be considered both as

   *   the point of intersection of two straight lines and

   *   the image point of a transformation.

3. be able to solve sets of simultaneous equations;

4. understand what is meant by consistency;

5. be able to give a geometrical interpretation of 3×3 simultaneous equations;

6. understand the effect of crushing transformations.

Elimination

Example

Solve the simultaneous equations

$$2x = 3y + 7 \qquad ①$$

$$5x - 4y = 14 \qquad ②$$

Solution

Step

$5① - 2②, \qquad 8y = 15y + 7$ — Eliminate x (or y).

$$-7y = 7$$

$$y = -1$$

In ①, $\qquad 2x = 4$ — Substitute the value of y back in an equation to give x.

$$\Rightarrow \quad x = 2$$

The solution is $x = 2$ and $y = -1$

1. Use elimination to solve

    (a) $2x + 5y = 11$ (b) $x - 3y = -4$

    $\quad\; 3x + y = 10$ $\quad\; 2x + 3y = 1$

    (c) $2x - 3y = 4$ (d) $5x = 2y - 4$

    $\quad\; 3x - 4y = 6$ $\quad\; 3x - y = -1$

    (e) $2y = 4x + 1$

    $\quad\; 5x + 3y = 7$

2. Use elimination to find the point of intersection of the two lines

    $$3y = 1 + 2x \quad \text{and} \quad 7y = 5x + 3$$

Destroying a dimension

1. If $A' = \mathbf{T}(A)$ where

    $$\mathbf{T} = \begin{bmatrix} -1 & -3 \\ 2 & -1 \end{bmatrix}$$

    (a) Sketch A'

    (b) Calculate

        (i) the area of A

        (ii) the area of A'

        (iii) $|\mathbf{T}|$, the
    determinant of $\mathbf{T}$

    Comment on the connection
    between your three answers.

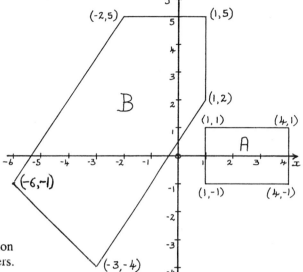

2. If $B' = \mathbf{S}(B)$ where $\mathbf{S} = \begin{bmatrix} 2 & -1 \\ -4 & 2 \end{bmatrix}$

    (a) Sketch B'.

    (b) Is $|\mathbf{S}|$ still the area scale factor?

    (c) What happens to any 2-dimensional object transformed by $\mathbf{S}$?

3. For the matrix transformation $\mathbf{R} = \begin{bmatrix} \dfrac{1}{5} & -\dfrac{2}{5} \\ -\dfrac{2}{5} & \dfrac{4}{5} \end{bmatrix}$

    (a) Choose a number of points and plot their images after they have been transformed
    by $\mathbf{R}$.

    (b) Calculate $|\mathbf{R}|$

    (c) What is the image space of $\mathbf{R}$, i.e. what is the image of all the points of the
    (x, y) plane?

    (d) How is the dimension of the image space related to the dimension of the original
    plane?

1.   (a)   Solve the equations

$$2x + ay = 6$$
$$bx + 8y = 9$$

(b)   Describe the nature of the solutions when $ab = 16$.

2.   Describe the transformation represented by the matrix $A = \begin{bmatrix} 3 & 2 \\ 6 & 4 \end{bmatrix}$

3.   Comment on the solution sets of

$$3x - y = 9$$
$$2x - 4y = 16$$
$$5x + 2y = a$$

for different values of a.

4.   Solve the following sets of equations

(a) $2x + 5y + z = 1$
       $4x - 3y - 2z = 8$
       $3x + 2y + 3z = 20$

(b) $2x + 5y + z = 1$
       $4x - 3y - 2z = 8$

5.   Find the value of k for which the planes

$$2x - y + 5z = 7$$
$$5x + 3y - z = 4$$
$$3x + 4y - 6z = k$$

form a sheaf.

6.   What is the condition for the planes $x + y = a$, $y + z = b$, $z - x = c$ to form a prism?

7.   Describe the configuration of the planes:

$$3x - y + 2z = 0$$
$$x + 4y + 3z = 2$$
$$6x - 2y + 4z = 5$$

4 *Identifying transformations*

4.1 Introduction

In earlier chapters you have seen how to find matrices representing simple transformations such as rotations and enlargements and also how to determine the transformations represented by certain matrices. However, not all matrices describe simple transformations and this chapter develops an approach that will enable you to describe the geometric effect of **any** 2 x 2 matrix.

(a) By illustrating the effect of the matrix $A = \begin{bmatrix} 1 & 0 \\ 0 & -1 \end{bmatrix}$ on the unit vectors i and j, describe the transformation represented by A.

(b) Illustrate the effect of the matrix $B = \begin{bmatrix} -1 & 2 \\ -2 & 3 \end{bmatrix}$ on the unit vectors i and j. Why is it not easy to determine the transformation represented by B?

(c) What else could you investigate to help discover the geometrical effects of B?

(d) How would it help if you knew that certain points or lines are fixed? How could you find these?

TASKSHEET 1 - *Finding clues*

> An *invariant point* is one which is its own image under a transformation.

In Tasksheet 1 you have seen how finding the invariant points of a transformation and the determinant of a matrix can help you describe the geometric nature of the transformation represented by the matrix. For example, a rotation has a single invariant point whereas a reflection has an infinite set of invariant points.

4.2   Fixed directions

The effect of the matrix $\mathbf{M} = \begin{bmatrix} 2 & 0 \\ 0 & 3 \end{bmatrix}$ is shown below

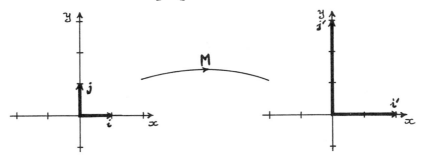

The matrix **M** represents a two-way stretch of factors 2 and 3 parallel to the x and y axes. Any point on the x-axis is a mapped onto another point on the x-axis and thus the x-axis is mapped onto itself. The x-axis is said to be invariant **as a whole**. In the same way, the y-axis is invariant **as a whole** under the transformation represented by **M**.

Tasksheet 2 investigates the invariant lines, or fixed directions, of other matrix transformations.

TASKSHEET 2 - *Fixed directions*

> An *invariant line* is one for which all points on the line map to points
> also on the line. The points on an invariant line need not be invariant
> points. Knowing the invariant lines, or fixed directions, helps you
> describe the transformation represented by a matrix.

Suppose that $\mathbf{e} = \begin{bmatrix} x \\ y \end{bmatrix}$ is a vector in a fixed direction of some matrix **M**. Then **Me** is parallel to **e** and so $\mathbf{Me} = \lambda\mathbf{e}$ for some number λ.

> A *fixed direction* or *eigenvector* of M is defined to be a non-zero
> vector e such that Me = λe for some number λ. The number λ
> is the stretch factor parallel to the eigenvector e and is called the
> *eigenvalue* of e.

> **(a)**   For a fixed direction, is the choice of eigenvector unique ?
>
> **(b)**   Can two parallel eigenvectors have different eigenvalues ?

Example 1

(a) Show that the lines $\mathbf{r} = \lambda \begin{bmatrix} 1 \\ 1 \end{bmatrix}$ and $\mathbf{r} = \lambda \begin{bmatrix} 5 \\ -3 \end{bmatrix}$ are invariant under the matrix transformation $\mathbf{M} = \begin{bmatrix} -2 & 5 \\ 3 & 0 \end{bmatrix}$.

(b) Describe the transformation represented by $\mathbf{M}$.

Solution

(a) Any point on $\mathbf{r} = \lambda \begin{bmatrix} 1 \\ 1 \end{bmatrix}$ has position vector $\begin{bmatrix} \lambda \\ \lambda \end{bmatrix}$

$$\begin{bmatrix} -2 & 5 \\ 3 & 0 \end{bmatrix} \begin{bmatrix} \lambda \\ \lambda \end{bmatrix} = \begin{bmatrix} 3\lambda \\ 3\lambda \end{bmatrix}$$

Thus, since its direction is unchanged, $\mathbf{r} = \lambda \begin{bmatrix} 1 \\ 1 \end{bmatrix}$ is invariant and all points on this line are mapped onto points on the line by a stretch of factor 3. Similarly, since

$$\begin{bmatrix} -2 & 5 \\ 3 & 0 \end{bmatrix} \begin{bmatrix} 5\lambda \\ -3\lambda \end{bmatrix} = \begin{bmatrix} -25\lambda \\ 15\lambda \end{bmatrix} = -5 \begin{bmatrix} 5\lambda \\ -3\lambda \end{bmatrix},$$

all points on the line $\mathbf{r} = \lambda \begin{bmatrix} 5 \\ -3 \end{bmatrix}$ are mapped onto points on the same line by a stretch of factor -5.

(b) $\mathbf{M}$ therefore represents a transformation with two fixed lines $\mathbf{r} = \lambda \begin{bmatrix} 1 \\ 1 \end{bmatrix}$ and $\mathbf{r} = \lambda \begin{bmatrix} 5 \\ -3 \end{bmatrix}$ with stretches of factors 3 and -5 respectively.

Exercise 1

1. Show that $\begin{bmatrix} -1 \\ 3 \end{bmatrix}$ and $\begin{bmatrix} 1 \\ -2 \end{bmatrix}$ are eigenvectors of the matrix $\begin{bmatrix} 0 & -1 \\ 6 & 5 \end{bmatrix}$.

   Hence describe the geometric effect of this matrix.

2. Investigate which of the vectors

   $$\begin{bmatrix} 2 \\ -1 \end{bmatrix}, \begin{bmatrix} -1 \\ -1 \end{bmatrix}, \begin{bmatrix} 1 \\ -1 \end{bmatrix} \text{ and } \begin{bmatrix} -2 \\ 3 \end{bmatrix}$$

   are eigenvectors of the matrix

   $$\begin{bmatrix} 8 & 10 \\ -5 & -7 \end{bmatrix}.$$

   Hence describe the transformation represented by the matrix.

3. Use the fact that the matrix $\begin{bmatrix} 0 & 1 \\ 1 & 0 \end{bmatrix}$ is a reflection in the line $y = x$ to write down its eigenvectors.

   Check your answer by multiplying the matrix by your eigenvectors.

4.3   Finding eigenvalues

You have seen that knowing the eigenvectors and eigenvalues of a matrix enables you to describe the matrix as a two-way stretch. It is natural to ask how to find these eigenvectors and eigenvalues.

Let $\mathbf{M} = \begin{bmatrix} 1 & -1 \\ 2 & 4 \end{bmatrix}$.

Suppose that $\mathbf{e} = \begin{bmatrix} x \\ y \end{bmatrix}$ is an eigenvector of $\mathbf{M}$ with eigenvalue λ.

then $\mathbf{Me} = \lambda\mathbf{e}$

$$\Rightarrow \quad \begin{bmatrix} 1 & -1 \\ 2 & 4 \end{bmatrix}\begin{bmatrix} x \\ y \end{bmatrix} = \lambda\begin{bmatrix} x \\ y \end{bmatrix}$$

$$\Rightarrow \quad \begin{bmatrix} 1 & -1 \\ 2 & 4 \end{bmatrix}\begin{bmatrix} x \\ y \end{bmatrix} - \begin{bmatrix} \lambda & 0 \\ 0 & \lambda \end{bmatrix}\begin{bmatrix} x \\ y \end{bmatrix} = \begin{bmatrix} 0 \\ 0 \end{bmatrix}$$

$$\Rightarrow \quad \begin{bmatrix} (1-\lambda) & -1 \\ 2 & 4-\lambda \end{bmatrix}\begin{bmatrix} x \\ y \end{bmatrix} = \begin{bmatrix} 0 \\ 0 \end{bmatrix}$$

In Chapter 3 you saw that, if there is a non-zero solution of this equation, then the determinant of the matrix is 0.

Thus, since any eigenvector is non zero,

$$\begin{vmatrix} 1-\lambda & -1 \\ 2 & 4-\lambda \end{vmatrix} = 0$$

$$\Rightarrow \quad (1-\lambda)(4-\lambda) - (-2) = 0$$

$$\Rightarrow \quad \lambda^2 - 5\lambda + 6 = 0$$

This equation, whose roots are the eigenvalues, is called the **characteristic equation.**

The equation $|\mathbf{A} - \lambda\mathbf{I}| = 0$ is called the characteristic equation of matrix $\mathbf{A}$.

Its roots are the eigenvalues of $\mathbf{A}$.

Exercise 2

1.   Find the characteristic equation and eigenvalues of the following matrices.

(a) $\begin{bmatrix} 3 & 2 \\ 1 & 2 \end{bmatrix}$ (b) $\begin{bmatrix} -2 & 2 \\ -1 & -5 \end{bmatrix}$

(c) $\begin{bmatrix} 2 & -3 \\ -4 & 6 \end{bmatrix}$ (d) $\begin{bmatrix} 0.75 & -0.5 \\ 0.5 & -0.5 \end{bmatrix}$

4.4 Finding eigenvectors

You can demonstrate the generality of the technique of Section 4.3 by considering a general matrix

$$\mathbf{M} = \begin{bmatrix} a & b \\ c & d \end{bmatrix}$$

If **e** is an eigenvector of **M** with eigenvalue λ then

$$\mathbf{Me} = \lambda \mathbf{e}, \quad \mathbf{e} \neq \mathbf{0}$$

$$\Rightarrow \quad \mathbf{Me} = \lambda \mathbf{Ie}$$

$$\Rightarrow \quad \mathbf{Me} - \lambda \mathbf{Ie} = \mathbf{0}$$

$$\Rightarrow \quad (\mathbf{M} - \lambda \mathbf{I})\mathbf{e} = \mathbf{0}$$

Since you know that $\mathbf{e} \neq \mathbf{0}$, the determinant of $(\mathbf{M} - \lambda \mathbf{I})$ must be 0.

$$\Rightarrow \quad |\mathbf{M} - \lambda \mathbf{I}| = 0$$

$$\Rightarrow \quad \begin{vmatrix} a-\lambda & b \\ c & d-\lambda \end{vmatrix} = 0$$

It is therefore easy to find the eigenvalues of a matrix. In Tasksheet 3 you will see how you can use these values to find the corresponding eigenvectors.

TASKSHEET 3 - *Finding eigenvectors*

For any matrix $\mathbf{M} = \begin{bmatrix} a & b \\ c & d \end{bmatrix}$, you can solve the characteristic equation

$$|\mathbf{M} - \lambda \mathbf{I}| = 0$$

to find the eigenvalues .

The eigenvector with eigenvalue λ can be found by considering the equation

$$\begin{bmatrix} a & b \\ c & d \end{bmatrix}\begin{bmatrix} x \\ y \end{bmatrix} = \lambda \begin{bmatrix} x \\ y \end{bmatrix}.$$

Example 2

Find the eigenvalues and eigenvectors of $\begin{bmatrix} 3 & 5 \\ 1 & -1 \end{bmatrix}$. Use your answers to describe the geometric effect of this transformation as fully as possible.

Solution

The characteristic equation is

$$\begin{vmatrix} 3-\lambda & 5 \\ 1 & -1-\lambda \end{vmatrix} = 0$$

$$\Rightarrow \quad (3-\lambda)(-1-\lambda) - 5 = 0$$

$$\Rightarrow \quad \lambda^2 - 2\lambda - 8 = 0$$

$$\Rightarrow \quad (\lambda - 4)(\lambda + 2) = 0$$

$$\Rightarrow \quad \lambda = 4 \text{ or } -2$$

For $\lambda = 4$,

$$\begin{bmatrix} 3-4 & 5 \\ 1 & -1-4 \end{bmatrix}\begin{bmatrix} x \\ y \end{bmatrix} = \begin{bmatrix} 0 \\ 0 \end{bmatrix}$$

$$\Rightarrow \begin{bmatrix} -x+5y \\ x-5y \end{bmatrix} = \begin{bmatrix} 0 \\ 0 \end{bmatrix}$$

A possible eigenvector is $\begin{bmatrix} 5 \\ 1 \end{bmatrix}$ although you could equally well choose $\begin{bmatrix} 10 \\ 2 \end{bmatrix}$ or $\begin{bmatrix} -5 \\ -1 \end{bmatrix}$ or ... because they are in the same direction as $\begin{bmatrix} 5 \\ 1 \end{bmatrix}$.

For $\lambda = -2$,

$$\begin{bmatrix} 3+2 & 5 \\ 1 & -1+2 \end{bmatrix}\begin{bmatrix} x \\ y \end{bmatrix} = \begin{bmatrix} 0 \\ 0 \end{bmatrix}$$

$$\Rightarrow \begin{bmatrix} 5x+5y \\ x+y \end{bmatrix} = \begin{bmatrix} 0 \\ 0 \end{bmatrix}$$

A possible eigenvector is $\begin{bmatrix} -1 \\ 1 \end{bmatrix}$.

M is a two-way stretch of factors 4 and –2 in directions $\begin{bmatrix} 5 \\ 1 \end{bmatrix}$ and $\begin{bmatrix} -1 \\ 1 \end{bmatrix}$, respectively.

To find the eigenvalues λ and eigenvectors e of a matrix $M = \begin{bmatrix} a & b \\ c & d \end{bmatrix}$

you need to solve the equation $Me = \lambda e$.

- Find the eigenvalues by solving the characteristic equation $|M - \lambda I| = 0$
- Substitute the eigenvalues into $\begin{bmatrix} a-\lambda & b \\ c & d-\lambda \end{bmatrix}\begin{bmatrix} x \\ y \end{bmatrix} = \begin{bmatrix} 0 \\ 0 \end{bmatrix}$

   to find the eigenvectors.

Exercise 3

1. You are given the eigenvalues for the matrices in this exercise. Use these values to find the eigenvectors. In each case draw a diagram showing the effect on the square $OABC$, where O is $(0, 0)$, A is $(1, 0)$, B is $(1, 1)$ and C is $(0, 1)$.

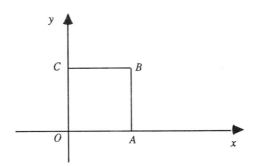

(a) $\begin{bmatrix} 3 & 2 \\ 1 & 2 \end{bmatrix}$ $\lambda = 1, 4$

(b) $\begin{bmatrix} -2 & 2 \\ -1 & -5 \end{bmatrix}$ $\lambda = -4, -3$

(c) $\begin{bmatrix} 2 & -3 \\ -4 & 6 \end{bmatrix}$ $\lambda = 0, 8$

(d) $\begin{bmatrix} 0.75 & -0.5 \\ 0.5 & -0.5 \end{bmatrix}$ $\lambda = -0.25, 0.5$

4.5 Diagonal matrices

In Section 4.4 you saw that the matrix

$$M = \begin{bmatrix} 3 & 5 \\ 1 & -1 \end{bmatrix}$$

represents a two-way stretch of factors 4 and -2 in the directions $\begin{bmatrix} 5 \\ 1 \end{bmatrix}$ and $\begin{bmatrix} -1 \\ 1 \end{bmatrix}$ respectively.

The diagonal matrix

$$D = \begin{bmatrix} 4 & 0 \\ 0 & -2 \end{bmatrix}$$

which represents a two-way stretch of factors 4 and -2 in the directions of the coordinate axes looks considerably simpler than M. For example, it is much easier to find $D^3 = \begin{bmatrix} 64 & 0 \\ 0 & -8 \end{bmatrix}$ than it is to find M^3. In fact, there is a close relationship between M and D which can be used to deduce results for M from corresponding results for D. This link is provided by the eigenvectors.

$$M \begin{bmatrix} 5 \\ 1 \end{bmatrix} = 4 \begin{bmatrix} 5 \\ 1 \end{bmatrix} = \begin{bmatrix} 20 \\ 4 \end{bmatrix} \quad \text{and} \quad M \begin{bmatrix} -1 \\ 1 \end{bmatrix} = -2 \begin{bmatrix} -1 \\ 1 \end{bmatrix} = \begin{bmatrix} 2 \\ -2 \end{bmatrix}$$

$$\text{So } M \begin{bmatrix} 5 & -1 \\ 1 & 1 \end{bmatrix} = \begin{bmatrix} 20 & 2 \\ 4 & -2 \end{bmatrix} = \begin{bmatrix} 5 & -1 \\ 1 & 1 \end{bmatrix} \begin{bmatrix} 4 & 0 \\ 0 & -2 \end{bmatrix}$$

$$\Rightarrow M \begin{bmatrix} 5 & -1 \\ 1 & -1 \end{bmatrix} = \begin{bmatrix} 5 & -1 \\ 1 & 1 \end{bmatrix} D.$$

Hence $MU = UD$ where U is the matrix whose columns are the eigenvectors and D is the diagonal matrix whose diagonal entries are the corresponding eigenvalues of M.

The equation

$$MU = UD$$

can be used to express M in terms of U and D.

$$\begin{aligned} MU &= UD \\ \Rightarrow \quad MUU^{-1} &= UDU^{-1} \\ \Rightarrow \quad M &= UDU^{-1} \end{aligned}$$

In expressing M in this form you will always have a choice regarding the order of the eigenvectors in the columns of U. It does not matter which order you choose providing that you use the same order for both U and D.

In Tasksheet 4 you will see how you can use the equation $\mathbf{M} = \mathbf{UDU}^{-1}$ to find $\mathbf{M}^2$ and other powers of $\mathbf{M}$.

 TASKSHEET 4 - *Powers of a matrix*

For the matrices $\mathbf{M} = \begin{bmatrix} 3 & 5 \\ 1 & -1 \end{bmatrix}$ and $\mathbf{D} = \begin{bmatrix} 4 & 0 \\ 0 & -2 \end{bmatrix}$ you have seen that $\mathbf{M} = \mathbf{UDU}^{-1}$

This relationship can be used to find powers of $\mathbf{M}$:

$$\mathbf{M}^2 = (\mathbf{UDU}^{-1})(\mathbf{UDU}^{-1})$$

$$= \mathbf{UD}(\mathbf{U}^{-1}\mathbf{U})\mathbf{DU}^{-1}$$

$$= \mathbf{UDIDU}^{-1}$$

$$= \mathbf{UD}^2\mathbf{U}^{-1}$$

Similarly,

$$\mathbf{M}^n = \mathbf{UD}^n\,\mathbf{U}^{-1}$$

Example 3

If $\mathbf{M} = \begin{bmatrix} 3 & 5 \\ 1 & -1 \end{bmatrix}$, find $\mathbf{M}^n$

Solution

$\mathbf{M}$ has eigenvalues 4 and -2 with corresponding eigenvectors $\begin{bmatrix} 5 \\ 1 \end{bmatrix}$ and $\begin{bmatrix} -1 \\ 1 \end{bmatrix}$.

So $\mathbf{D} = \begin{bmatrix} 4 & 0 \\ 0 & -2 \end{bmatrix}$

and $\mathbf{U} = \begin{bmatrix} 5 & -1 \\ 1 & 1 \end{bmatrix} \Rightarrow \mathbf{U}^{-1} = \frac{1}{6}\begin{bmatrix} 1 & 1 \\ -1 & 5 \end{bmatrix}$

$\mathbf{M}^n = \mathbf{UD}^n\,\mathbf{U}^{-1}$

$$\Rightarrow \mathbf{M}^n = \begin{bmatrix} 5 & -1 \\ 1 & 1 \end{bmatrix} \times \begin{bmatrix} 4^n & 0 \\ 0 & (-2)^n \end{bmatrix} \times \frac{1}{6}\begin{bmatrix} 1 & 1 \\ -1 & 5 \end{bmatrix}$$

$$\Rightarrow \mathbf{M}^n = \frac{4^n}{6}\begin{bmatrix} 5 & 5 \\ 1 & 1 \end{bmatrix} + \frac{(-2)^n}{6}\begin{bmatrix} 1 & -5 \\ -1 & 5 \end{bmatrix}$$

In general:

Exercise 4

1. For each of the matrices **M** below:

    (i)   write **M** in the form $\mathbf{UDU^{-1}}$;

    (ii) give a geometrical description of the transformation represented by **M**;

    (a) $\begin{bmatrix} 2 & 1 \\ 4 & -1 \end{bmatrix}$ (b) $\begin{bmatrix} 1 & 3 \\ 2 & -4 \end{bmatrix}$

    (c) $\begin{bmatrix} 1 & 6 \\ 6 & 1 \end{bmatrix}$ (d) $\begin{bmatrix} 1 & -1 \\ \frac{1}{3} & -\frac{1}{6} \end{bmatrix}$

2. A linear transformation with matrix **M** is a two-way stretch in the directions $y = 3x$ and $2y = -x$ with stretch factors $\frac{1}{3}$ and 2.

    (a) Find the eigenvectors of this transformation and write down matrices **U** and **D** which satisfy the equation $\mathbf{M} = \mathbf{UDU^{-1}}$.

    (b) Find the matrix **M**.

4.6   Transition matrices

In Chapter 1 you met transition matrices which described a process known as a **stochastic process** in which the probability of a subsequent event depends only upon the outcome of the preceding event.

For example, suppose that you classify the weather on any particular day as sunny (S) or cloudy (C). It is reasonable to assume that the weather on any day depends to some extent on the weather on the previous day.

You can model this situation as follows:

(i)   if today is sunny then suppose the probabilities that it will be sunny or cloudy tomorrow are 0.7 and 0.3 respectively,

and

(ii)   if today is cloudy then suppose the probabilities that it will be sunny or cloudy tomorrow are 0.2 and 0.8 respectively.

The transition matrix which describes this is

$$\mathbf{T} = \begin{array}{c} \\ S \\ C \end{array} \begin{array}{cc} S & C \\ \left[\begin{array}{cc} 0.7 & 0.2 \\ 0.3 & 0.8 \end{array} \right] \end{array}$$

How can you determine what is likely to happen

(a)   **during the next few days;**

(b)   **in the long term?**

   TASKSHEET 5 - *Transition matrices*

It can be shown that any 2 x 2 probability matrix has an eigenvalue equal to 1 and that the corresponding eigenvector (with elements adding to 1) describes the long term probabilities: this vector is sometimes known as the **steady state vector.**

4.7   Inverse matrices

In Section 4.5 you met a method of finding powers of any 2 x 2 matrix for which you knew two non-parallel eigenvectors. Not all matrices have such eigenvectors, for example, any eigenvector of the simple matrix $\begin{bmatrix} 1 & 1 \\ 0 & 1 \end{bmatrix}$ is of the form $k \begin{bmatrix} 1 \\ 0 \end{bmatrix}$.

> **Show that any eigenvector is of the form $k \begin{bmatrix} 1 \\ 0 \end{bmatrix}$.**

In this section you will investigate a remarkable theorem which is true for **any** square matrix of **any** size.

> (a)   Show that the characteristic equation of
>
> $$M = \begin{bmatrix} 4 & -5 \\ 1 & -2 \end{bmatrix} \quad \text{is}$$
>
> $$\lambda^2 - 2\lambda - 3 = 0.$$
>
> (b)   Find $M^2 - 2M - 3I$.
>
> (c)   Comment on your answers to parts (a) and (b).

   TASKSHEET 6 - *Cayley-Hamilton theorem*

The result that a matrix **M** will satisfy its own characteristic equation is known as the **Cayley-Hamilton theorem.** You have only proved this result for a 2 x 2 matrix which can be expressed as UDU^{-1} for a diagonal matrix **D**. The result is however true for any square matrix.

> **If a 2 x 2 matrix M has characteristic equation**
> $a\lambda^2 + b\lambda + c = 0$ **then M satisfies the equation**
> $aM^2 + bM + cI = 0$

The Cayley-Hamilton theorem can be used to find the inverse M^{-1} since

$$aM + b + cM^{-1} = 0$$

and the theorem can be used to find successive powers, since

$$aM^3 + bM^2 + cM = 0$$
$$aM^4 + bM^3 + cM^2 = 0 \text{ etc.}$$

After working through this chapter you should:

1. be able to find the eigenvalues and eigenvectors of a 2 x 2 matrix;

2. appreciate the geometrical significance of the eigenvalues and eigenvectors of a matrix;

3. be able to express a matrix in diagonal form, $M = UDU^{-1}$;

4. be able to find powers of a matrix using the diagonal form;

5. be able to use the Cayley-Hamilton theorem to find powers of a matrix including its inverse;

6. appreciate the significance of eigenvalues and eigenvectors in the theory of probability matrices.

Finding clues

1. This question investigates the transformation represented by the matrix

    $$\mathbf{M} = \begin{bmatrix} -1 & 2 \\ -2 & 3 \end{bmatrix}$$

    (a) Find the determinant of **M**. What does this tell you about the transformation represented by **M**?

    (b) Find the images of the points $(3, 1)$, $(-2, -2)$, $(4, 1)$, $(7, 7)$ and $(3, 5)$.

    (c) Which points in part (b) are **invariant** - i.e. do not move?

    (d) If a point (x, y) is invariant then

    $$\mathbf{M} \begin{bmatrix} x \\ y \end{bmatrix} = \begin{bmatrix} x \\ y \end{bmatrix}$$

    i.e. $\begin{bmatrix} -1 & 2 \\ -2 & 3 \end{bmatrix}\begin{bmatrix} x \\ y \end{bmatrix} = \begin{bmatrix} x \\ y \end{bmatrix}$

    Use this condition to write down two equations involving x and y, and hence find all points which are invariant under **M**.

    (e) By considering the invariant points explain why **M** cannot represent

    (i) a rotation; (ii) an enlargement;

    (iii) a two-way stretch.

    (f) Draw a diagram showing the invariant points of the transformation.

    Choose several points **P** with images **P′** and draw the vectors $\overrightarrow{\mathbf{PP'}}$ on your diagram. Describe, as fully as you can, the geometric effect of the transformation represented by **M**.

(continued)

2.   (a)   Find $\mathbf{M} \begin{bmatrix} 0 \\ 0 \end{bmatrix}$ for any matrix $\mathbf{M} = \begin{bmatrix} a & b \\ c & d \end{bmatrix}$.

       (b)   What is the image of the origin under the translation through $\begin{bmatrix} a \\ b \end{bmatrix}$?

             Explain why a matrix can never represent a translation.

       (c)   If a matrix represents a rotation, what can you say about the centre of the
             rotation?

       (d)   If a matrix represents a reflection, what can you say about the mirror line?

       (e)   What is the area scale factor for a rotation and for a reflection? What is the
             connection with the determinants of the matrices of these transformations?

3.   (a) $\mathbf{M} = \begin{bmatrix} -0.6 & 0.8 \\ 0.8 & 0.6 \end{bmatrix}$.

             Show that all points of the form $(t, 2t)$ are invariant under the transformation
             represented by the matrix $\mathbf{M}$.

       (b)   (i)   Write down a list of transformations which cannot be represented by the
                    matrix $\mathbf{M}$;

             (ii)   Write down a list of transformations which might be represented by the
                    matrix $\mathbf{M}$.

       (c)   Find the determinant of the matrix $\mathbf{M}$. What transformation is represented by $\mathbf{M}$?

4.   Show that points of the form $(2t, -t)$ are invariant under the transformation represented
       by the matrix

             $\begin{bmatrix} 0.6 & -0.8 \\ -0.8 & -0.6 \end{bmatrix}$.

       Investigate this transformation.

Fixed directions

1.　(a)　Find the images of (1, 1), (5, 5) and (–7, –7) under the matrix transformation

$$M = \begin{bmatrix} 1 & 3 \\ -2 & 6 \end{bmatrix}$$

　　(b)　Find the image of the point (t, t) under **M**. What can you conclude about the image of the line

$$\mathbf{r} = t\begin{bmatrix} 1 \\ 1 \end{bmatrix}$$

　　(c)　Show that the line $\mathbf{r} = t\begin{bmatrix} 3 \\ 2 \end{bmatrix}$ is also invariant.

　　(d)　Describe the geometric effect of **M** as fully as you can.

2.　(a)　Show that each point on the line $\mathbf{r} = t\begin{bmatrix} 3 \\ 4 \end{bmatrix}$ is invariant under the matrix transformation

$$\begin{bmatrix} -0.28 & 0.96 \\ 0.96 & 0.28 \end{bmatrix}.$$

　　(b)　Show that the line $\mathbf{r} = t\begin{bmatrix} -4 \\ 3 \end{bmatrix}$ is also invariant.

　　(c)　Describe the transformation.

3.　(a)　Investigate the images of the lines

$$\mathbf{r} = t\begin{bmatrix} 2 \\ 1 \end{bmatrix} \quad \text{and} \quad \mathbf{r} = t\begin{bmatrix} -1 \\ 2 \end{bmatrix}$$

　　　　under the matrix transformation $\begin{bmatrix} 0.8 & 0.4 \\ 0.4 & 0.2 \end{bmatrix}.$

　　(b)　Describe the geometric effect of this matrix as fully as you can.

Finding eigenvectors

1. (a) Show that the vector $\begin{bmatrix} 3t \\ t \end{bmatrix}$ satisfies the equation $x - 3y = 0$ for all values of t.

   By putting $t = 1, 2, -2$ find particular vectors which satisfy the equation.

   (b) By first writing x in terms of y, find a vector of the form $\begin{bmatrix} kt \\ t \end{bmatrix}$ which satisfies the equation $4x + 5y = 0$.

   By putting $t = 4, 7, -4$ find particular vectors which satisfy the equation.

   (c) Find three vectors which satisfy the equation $3x + 2y = 0$.

2. You have seen that the matrix

   $$\mathbf{M} = \begin{bmatrix} 1 & -1 \\ 2 & 4 \end{bmatrix}$$

   has eigenvalues 2 and 3.

   (a) By writing $\begin{bmatrix} 1 & -1 \\ 2 & 4 \end{bmatrix}\begin{bmatrix} x \\ y \end{bmatrix} = 2\begin{bmatrix} x \\ y \end{bmatrix}$

   and obtaining equations in x and y, find an eigenvector corresponding to the eigenvalue 2.

   (b) Find an eigenvector corresponding to the eigenvalue 3.

   (c) Describe the geometric effect of $\mathbf{M}$ as fully as you can.

3. Find the eigenvalues and eigenvectors of the matrix

   $$\begin{bmatrix} 2 & 3 \\ 4 & 1 \end{bmatrix}.$$

   Hence describe the geometric effect of the matrix.

4. What happens when you try to find the eigenvalues of the matrix

   $$\begin{bmatrix} 2 & -3 \\ 4 & 1 \end{bmatrix}.$$

   What can you say about the geometric effect of this matrix?

Powers of a matrix

1.   If $M = UDU^{-1}$, explain why $M^2 = UD^2U^{-1}$.

Find a similar expression for M^n.

2.   Let $M = \begin{bmatrix} 4 & -3 \\ 2 & -1 \end{bmatrix}$.

(a)   Find the eigenvalues and eigenvectors of M.

(b)   Express M in the form UDU^{-1}.

(c)   Use the result of question 1 to find M^{54}. You may leave powers of 2 in your answer.

3.   Let $M = \begin{bmatrix} \dfrac{1}{2} & \dfrac{1}{3} \\ \dfrac{1}{2} & \dfrac{2}{3} \end{bmatrix}$.

(a)   Express M in the form UDU^{-1}.

(b)   What can you say about D^n as n tends to $+\infty$?

(c)   What can you say about M^n as n tends to $+\infty$?

Transition matrices

1.   You have met the transition matrix **T** modelling the weather:

$$\mathbf{T} = \begin{matrix} & \text{S} & \text{C} \\ \text{S} \\ \text{C} \end{matrix} \begin{bmatrix} 0.7 & 0.2 \\ 0.3 & 0.8 \end{bmatrix}$$

(a)   Express **T** in the form $\mathbf{UDU}^{-1}$, where **D** is a diagonal matrix.

(b)   Find $\mathbf{D}^n$, and say what happens as n tends to $+\infty$.

(c)   What happens to $\mathbf{T}^n \begin{bmatrix} 1 \\ 0 \end{bmatrix}$ as n tends to $+\infty$?

(d)   If the first day is sunny what is the approximate probability that the 100th day will also be sunny?

Would your answer be different if the first day had been cloudy, or if you had known nothing about the weather on the first day?

2.   A machine produces compact discs, some of which are faulty. If the machine produces a good disc then the chances that the next disc is also good are 90%, but if the machine produces a faulty disc then the chances that the next disc is good are only 20%.

Write down the transition matrix and find the long term probability that a particular disc is good.

3.   The transition matrices in questions 1 and 2 both have eigenvalues of 1. Find the corresponding eigenvectors in the form $\begin{bmatrix} a \\ b \end{bmatrix}$, where $a + b = 1$.

Comment on the eigenvectors and the corresponding long term probabilities.

Cayley-Hamilton theorem

1. (a) Show that the characteristic equation of the matrix

$$M = \begin{bmatrix} 2 & -1 \\ 3 & 4 \end{bmatrix}$$

is $\lambda^2 - 6\lambda + 11 = 0$.

(b) Show that the matrix M satisfies this equation i.e. show that

$$M^2 - 6M + 11I = \begin{bmatrix} 0 & 0 \\ 0 & 0 \end{bmatrix} = 0$$

2. Suppose that a 2×2 matrix M has characteristic equation

$$a\lambda^2 + b\lambda + c = 0.$$

(a) If λ_1 and λ_2 are eigenvalues of M explain why

$$a\lambda_1^2 + b\lambda_1 + c = 0 \text{ and } a\lambda_2^2 + b\lambda_2 + c = 0.$$

(b) If $D = \begin{bmatrix} \lambda_1 & 0 \\ 0 & \lambda_2 \end{bmatrix}$, find D^2.

(c) If $M = UDU^{-1}$ show that $aM^2 + bM + cI$ can be rewritten as

$$U(aD^2 + bD + cI)U^{-1}$$

and hence prove that $aM^2 + bM + cI = 0$.

This result is known as the Cayley-Hamilton theorem.

3. M is the matrix $\begin{bmatrix} 2 & -1 \\ 3 & 1 \end{bmatrix}$.

(a) Show that $M^2 - 3M + 5I = 0$.

(b) Find the inverse of M, M^{-1}, by multiplying both sides of the equation in (a) by M^{-1}

(c) Check your answer by calculating $M^{-1}M$.

(d) Use equation (a) to find M^2.

(e) Show that $M^3 - 3M^2 + 5M = 0$ and hence find M^3.

4. If $M = \begin{bmatrix} 2 & -1 \\ 3 & 4 \end{bmatrix}$, find   (a) M^{-1} (b) M^3.

1.   (a)   Explain why any 2 x 2 probability matrix can be written in the form

$$\mathbf{T} = \begin{bmatrix} 1-a & b \\ a & 1-b \end{bmatrix} ,$$

where a, b lie between 0 and 1 inclusive.

(b)   By considering $| \mathbf{T} - \lambda \mathbf{I} | = 0$ show that one eigenvalue must equal 1 and that the other must have modulus less than or equal to 1.

(c)   Express $\mathbf{T}$ in the form $\mathbf{UDU}^{-1}$ and explain what happens to $\mathbf{T}^n$ as n becomes very large.
Explain the significance of your answer in terms of probabilities.

Question 2 shows how the results of this chapter carry over to 3 x 3 matrices. They can be generalised for any n x n matrix.

2.   (a)   Verify that the vectors

$$\begin{bmatrix} 1 \\ 0 \\ -1 \end{bmatrix}, \begin{bmatrix} 2 \\ -1 \\ 0 \end{bmatrix} \text{ and } \begin{bmatrix} 0 \\ 1 \\ -1 \end{bmatrix}$$

are eigenvectors of the matrix $\mathbf{M} = \begin{bmatrix} 3 & 2 & 2 \\ 1 & 4 & 1 \\ -2 & -4 & -1 \end{bmatrix} .$

Find the corresponding eigenvalues.

Hence describe the geometric effect of the transformation described by the matrix $\mathbf{M}$.

(b)   If $\mathbf{U} = \begin{bmatrix} 1 & 2 & 0 \\ 0 & -1 & 1 \\ -1 & 0 & -1 \end{bmatrix}$ verify that $\mathbf{U}^{-1} = \begin{bmatrix} -1 & -2 & -2 \\ 1 & 1 & 1 \\ 1 & 2 & 1 \end{bmatrix} .$

Hence write $\mathbf{M}$ in the form $\mathbf{UDU}^{-1}$, where $\mathbf{D}$ is a diagonal matrix.

Use your answer to find $\mathbf{M}^7$.

(c)   Show that the eigenvalues satisfy the equation

$$\lambda^3 - 6\lambda^2 + 11\lambda - 6 = 0$$

Assuming that the matrix $\mathbf{M}$ also satisfies this equation, find $\mathbf{M}^{-1}$.

(continued)

3.   Suppose that an $n \times n$ matrix $\mathbf{M}$ has n distinct eigenvalues λ_1 , $\ldots$, λ_n corresponding to the n eigenvectors $\mathbf{e}_1$, $\ldots$, $\mathbf{e}_n$.

(a)   If $\mathbf{M}$ has characteristic equation

$$a_n \lambda^n + a_{n-1} \lambda^{n-1} + \ldots + a_1 \lambda + a_0 = 0$$

explain why

$$a_n \lambda_i^n + a_{n-1} \lambda_i^{n-1} + \ldots + a_1 \lambda_i + a_0 = 0$$

for all values of $i = 1, 2, \ldots, n$.

(b)   Given that $\mathbf{M}$ can be written in the form $\mathbf{UDU}^{-1}$ show that

$$a_n \mathbf{M}^n + a_{n-1} \mathbf{M}^{n-1} + \ldots + a_1 \mathbf{M} + a_0 \mathbf{I}$$

can be written as

$$\mathbf{U}\,(a_n \mathbf{D}^n + a_{n-1} \mathbf{D}^{n-1} + \ldots + a_1 \mathbf{D} + a_0 \mathbf{I}\,)\mathbf{U}^{-1}$$

and hence show that $\mathbf{M}$ satisfies its own characteristic equation.

5 *Numerical techniques*

5.1 Gaussian elimination

A major application of matrix theory is the solution of large numbers of simultaneous equations. The fact that a matrix contains only the coefficients of the equations without any superfluous information makes it a neat and efficient entity with which to work. In this chapter you will study various numerical techniques and examine the advantages and disadvantages of each, including problems that can arise because of rounding or when the coefficients of the variables are imprecise.

The solution of problems in applied mathematics often involves simultaneous equations in a large number of variables. An example is considered on Tasksheet 1.

TASKSHEET 1 - *Temperature distribution*

In Chapter 3 you met the elimination method for solving three equations in three unknowns such as

$$3x_1 + 7x_2 - 2x_3 = 4 \qquad ①$$

$$2x_1 - 9x_2 + 4x_3 = 5 \qquad ②$$

$$7x_1 - 5x_2 + 2x_3 = 8 \qquad ③$$

(a) **How would you solve these equations?**

(b) **Describe how you would solve the set of simultaneous equations given above systematically, for example by writing a computer program.**

(c) **Does your method extend to the solution of 4 x 4 sets?**

(d) **What is the effect of having rounded data rather than exact integers for the coefficients in the equations? Can you suggest ways of improving the precision?**

The method of systematic elimination is dependent upon the use of **row operations**. It relies on the principle that the solution to a set of equations is unchanged by:

- multiplying a row by a non-zero constant;

- adding a multiple of one row to another or subtracting a multiple of one row from another.

The discussion point developed an **algorithm** for the solution of **any** set of equations. The algorithm makes use of the formal ideas of row operations and is due to the famous early 19th century mathematician, Carl Friedrich Gauss. The method can be refined into a tabular form and is known as **Gaussian elimination.**

Example 1

Solve the equations

$$4x_1 + 3x_2 + x_3 = 7$$

$$2x_1 - x_2 - 5x_3 = -15$$

$$x_1 + 2x_2 - 3x_3 = -1$$

Solution

In tabular form:

Operation		x_1	x_2	x_3	c	Row no.
Coefficients	⎰⎱	4	3	1	7	①
		2	-1	-5	-15	②
		1	2	-3	-1	③
②-0.5 ①		0	-2.5	-5.5	-18.5	④
③-0.25①		0	1.25	-3.25	-2.75	⑤
⑤+0.5 ④		0	0	-6	-12	⑥

It is now easy to use back substitution to obtain, successively,

In ⑥ , $\qquad -6x_3 = -12 \quad \Rightarrow x_3 = 2$

In ⑤ , $\quad 1.25x_2 - 3.25x_3 = -2.75 \Rightarrow x_2 = 3$

In ① , $\quad 4x_1 + 3x_2 + x_3 = 7 \qquad \Rightarrow x_1 = -1$

$$\boxed{\text{Show that } x_2 = 3}$$

In eliminating x_1, the coefficient 4 was used to reduce the coefficients 2 and 1 to zero. To eliminate x_2, the coefficient -2.5 fulfilled a similar role, At each stage, these important coefficients are referred to as **pivots**. Their full importance will be discussed in a later section when the accuracy of the method is considered.

Until recently Gaussian elimination was a very popular method of solving sets of equations. Nowadays most large sets of equations are solved by computer or calculators using alternative techniques and there is less need for this formal systematic approach.

> **In order to solve a set of n equations in n unknowns using Gaussian elimination:**
>
> (a) choose the coefficient of the first variable in the first equation as the pivot;
>
> (b) using the pivot, eliminate this first variable from the remaining equations by subtracting multiples of the first equation;
>
> (c) repeat steps (a) and (b) to eliminate the second variable;
>
> (d) continue until just one variable remains;
>
> (e) use back substitution to find each variable in turn.

Exercise 1

1. Use the tabular method of Gaussian elimination with back substitution to solve the simultaneous equations:

$$8x_1 + 2x_2 + 4x_3 = 26$$

$$4x_1 + 5x_2 - x_3 = 0$$

$$2x_1 - 3x_2 + 5x_3 = 22$$

2. Solve the following equations using Gaussian elimination:

(a) $9x_1 + 5x_2 - 3x_3 = 11$

$5x_1 + 3x_2 + 2x_3 = 6$

$3x_1 - 8x_2 + x_3 = 1$

(b) $4.56x_1 - 7.59x_2 + 2.61x_3 = 0.67$

$1.52x_1 + 5.77x_2 + 4.30x_3 = 9.72$

$0.57x_1 + 9.84x_2 + 2.24x_3 = 5.45$

5.2　LU decomposition

Computing techniques for solving large sets of equations often rely on matrix methods. Of the many matrix methods employed, LU decomposition is one of the most popular, since it is both fast and efficient. You have already seen that back substitution is a quick and easy method which is readily programmed. Back substitution can be used when the matrix of coefficients is triangular. The next tasksheet shows how a general square matrix can be expressed as a product of two triangular matrices, one with zeros above the leading diagonal (a lower triangular matrix) and the other with zeros below the leading diagonal (an upper triangular matrix). Hence the name, LU decomposition, which is short for Lower-Upper.

　　　TASKSHEET 2 - *Triangular matrices*

> To solve the system of equations
>
> $$Ax = b,$$
>
> express A as LU, where L and U are lower and upper triangular matrices respectively.
>
> To solve $L(Ux) = b$ it is sufficient to solve $Ly = b$ and $Ux = y$.

Example 2

Solve the simultaneous equations

$$2x_1 + 3x_2 - x_3 = 9$$

$$-2x_1 + x_2 + 3x_3 = 7$$

$$-6x_1 - x_2 + 12x_3 = 15$$

Solution

For LU decomposition, triangular matrices must be found such that:

$$\begin{bmatrix} 2 & 3 & -1 \\ -2 & 1 & 3 \\ -6 & -1 & 12 \end{bmatrix} = \begin{bmatrix} 1 & 0 & 0 \\ * & 1 & 0 \\ * & * & 1 \end{bmatrix} \begin{bmatrix} * & * & * \\ 0 & * & * \\ 0 & 0 & * \end{bmatrix}$$

The top row of the upper triangular matrix is simply the top row of the original matrix. The remaining coefficients can be found by solving simple equations.

$$\begin{bmatrix} 2 & 3 & -1 \\ -2 & 1 & 3 \\ -6 & -1 & 12 \end{bmatrix} = \begin{bmatrix} 1 & 0 & 0 \\ l & 1 & 0 \\ m & n & 1 \end{bmatrix} \begin{bmatrix} 2 & 3 & -1 \\ 0 & u & v \\ 0 & 0 & w \end{bmatrix}$$

Second row of product:

$$2l \quad = -2 \Rightarrow l = -1$$

$$3l + u = \quad 1 \Rightarrow u = 4$$

$$-l + v = \quad 3 \Rightarrow v = 2$$

Third row of product:

$$2m \qquad = -6 \Rightarrow m = -3$$

$$3m + nu \quad = -1 \Rightarrow n = 2$$

$$-m + nv + w = \quad 12 \Rightarrow w = 5$$

Then $\begin{bmatrix} 1 & 0 & 0 \\ -1 & 1 & 0 \\ -3 & 2 & 1 \end{bmatrix} \begin{bmatrix} y_1 \\ y_2 \\ y_3 \end{bmatrix} = \begin{bmatrix} 9 \\ 7 \\ 15 \end{bmatrix} \Rightarrow \mathbf{y} = \begin{bmatrix} 9 \\ 16 \\ 10 \end{bmatrix}$

$$\begin{bmatrix} 2 & 3 & -1 \\ 0 & 4 & 2 \\ 0 & 0 & 5 \end{bmatrix} \begin{bmatrix} x_1 \\ x_2 \\ x_3 \end{bmatrix} = \begin{bmatrix} 9 \\ 16 \\ 10 \end{bmatrix} \Rightarrow \mathbf{x} = \begin{bmatrix} 1 \\ 3 \\ 2 \end{bmatrix}$$

$x_1 = 1, \; x_2 = 3, \; x_3 = 2$

Exercise 2

1. Use LU decomposition to solve the simultaneous equations:

$$3x_1 - 2x_2 + 2x_3 = 14$$
$$6x_1 - 2x_2 + 4x_3 = 20$$
$$- 2x_2 + x_3 = 8$$

2. Use LU decomposition to solve the 4 x 4 equations:

$$3x_1 \qquad + x_3 - 2x_4 = 1$$
$$x_1 + 2x_2 + \qquad 5x_4 = 17$$
$$4x_1 - x_2 + 3x_3 \qquad = 11$$
$$3x_2 - x_3 + x_4 = 2$$

5.3   An iterative approach

The LU method of solving simultaneous equations is an exact method and will give a unique solution if one exists. It is also quite efficient, though solving a set of 100 simultaneous equations in 100 unknowns can require around 30 000 arithmetic operations. A further complication is that all the coefficients need to be stored and manipulated at the same time.

An alternative way of solving simultaneous equations is to take an iterative approach which, if well chosen, will give the desired accuracy with fewer operations. As with other iterative methods however, it might fail to converge or might converge only slowly. The most widely used iterative method is also due to Gauss, and is known as the **Gauss Seidel** method.

   TASKSHEET 3 - *Gauss Seidel*

Example 3

Use the Gauss Seidel method to solve the equations

$$2x + y = 7$$

$$-x + 3y = 6$$

to an accuracy of 2 decimal places.

Solution

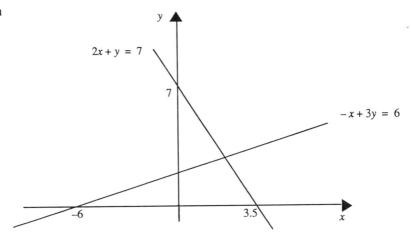

From the graph, an initial approximation is $x_0 = 2$, $y_0 = 3$

90

The two iterative formulas are

$$x_{n+1} = \frac{7 - y_n}{2} \qquad \text{and} \qquad y_{n+1} = \frac{x_{n+1} + 6}{3}$$

Then $x_1 = \dfrac{7-3}{2} = 2$ $\qquad\qquad\qquad$ $y_1 = \dfrac{2+6}{3} = 2.67$

$x_2 = 2.167$ $\qquad\qquad\qquad$ $y_2 = 2.722$

$x_3 = 2.1389$ $\qquad\qquad\qquad$ $y_3 = 2.7130$

$x_4 = 2.1435$ $\qquad\qquad\qquad$ $y_4 = 2.7145$

$x \approx 2.14$ and $y \approx 2.71$, to 2 decimal places

> **In Example 3, the number of decimal places recorded in the answer increased at each stage of the iteration. Can you suggest why this is a sensible policy in iterative problems?**

Exercise 3

Use the Gauss Seidel method to solve the following sets of equations.

1. $8x + 2y = 3$

   $2x - 5y = -5$

2. $20x - 3y - z = 4$

   $2x + 5y + 3z = 8$

   $4x - y + 7z = 11$

5.4   Implementing the techniques

In practice, the methods described in earlier sections are implemented by means of computer programs. Many 'real' sets of equations arise with non-exact coefficients, due to inherent experimental inaccuracy or simply because of rounding. However, the effect of rounding errors can spread throughout a calculation. Since the solution of equations may involve tens of thousands of arithmetic operations it is important to consider how these rounding errors affect the accuracy of the final answer and to examine ways of minimising their effect.

TASKSHEET 4 - *Using computer packages*

On the tasksheet you saw the need for a careful choice of pivot when applying Gaussian elimination. There is a similar need for a careful choice of order of equations when applying LU decomposition.

For example, $\begin{bmatrix} 0 & 0 \\ 1 & 0 \end{bmatrix}$ **cannot** be expressed in LU form with 1's on the diagonal of L,

whereas $\begin{bmatrix} 1 & 0 \\ 0 & 0 \end{bmatrix} = \begin{bmatrix} 1 & 0 \\ 0 & 1 \end{bmatrix} \begin{bmatrix} 1 & 0 \\ 0 & 0 \end{bmatrix}$

For LU decomposition you cannot rearrange the equations as you go along. The best you can reasonably do is to initially arrange the equations so that elements on the diagonal are relatively large in magnitude, i.e. ensure that there is a strong leading diagonal.

Some guidelines for a choice of which technique to use are given below.

Method	Use for	Precautions
Row operations	Small sets with integer coefficients	No special ones
Gaussian elimination	Small sets performed by hand	Arrange the equations so that each pivot is the largest available at that stage
LU decomposition	Large sets by computer	Ensure a strong leading diagonal
Gauss Seidel	Very large sets especially with many coefficients zero.	Ensure a strong leading diagonal

5.5   Ill conditioning

As you saw in the previous section, rounding of coefficients leads to errors in the solution. In some cases the errors inherent in the coefficients can lead to such instability in the final solution that any attempt to solve the equations must be carried out very carefully and must include an assessment of the error involved. Such a set of equations is described as being **ill conditioned**.

   TASKSHEET 5 - *Ill conditioning*

Solving a pair of simultaneous equations is equivalent to finding the point of intersection of two lines. Ill conditioning occurs when the two lines have very similar gradients; a small change in the coefficients can then lead to a wild fluctuation in the solution. Most sets of equations arise from applications where measurements have been taken. Consequently, the coefficients are then written to a prescribed degree of accuracy. If the equations are ill conditioned then great care is necessary!

Example 4

Show that the following equations, whose coefficients have been rounded to 1 decimal place, are ill conditioned:

$$7.6x + 2.9y = 2.1 \qquad ①$$

$$6.1x + 2.4y = 5.2 \qquad ②$$

Solution

Since the coefficients are written to one decimal place, the x coefficient in ① can be any number in the range 7.55 to 7.65. The other coefficients are similarly only known to within ± 0.05. Just two of the many possibilities for the equations are:

(a) $\qquad 7.65x + 2.85y = 2.1$

$\qquad 6.05x + 2.45y = 5.2$

which have solution $x = -6.5, \ y = 18.05$

(b) $\qquad 7.55x + 2.95y = 2.1$

$\qquad 6.15x + 2.35y = 5.2$

which have solution $x = 26.0, \ y = -65.9$

The small variation in the coefficients inherent in rounding to one decimal place causes a huge variation in the solution. The equations are therefore ill conditioned.

After working through this chapter you should:

1. recognise problems which give rise to large sets of simultaneous equations;

2. be able to solve a set of 3 x 3 or 4 x 4 simultaneous equations using row operations or the method of Gaussian elimination;

3. be able to solve sets of simultaneous equations using LU decomposition;

4. be able to solve sets of simultaneous equations using the Gauss Seidel method;

5. be able to choose a technique appropriate to the set of equations to be solved;

6. be able to recognise a set of ill conditioned equations in the 2 x 2 case.

Temperature distribution

This tasksheet examines the way simultaneous equations can be used to solve a sophisticated mathematical problem. The task is to find the temperature distribution across a thin plate whose edges are maintained at a constant temperature and whose faces are insulated.

For example:

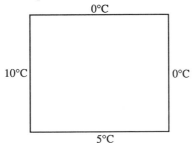

In time, the temperature distribution through the plate will reach a steady state.

On this tasksheet, a large set of equations will be obtained. The methods to be developed in this chapter will later be applied to solve these equations and thus the problem.

1. The above problem is a model of a real situation. What assumptions have been made in the model? Are they sensible assumptions?

The mathematical technique to be used involves dividing the plate into a series of square meshes:

(i) 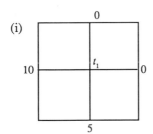   (ii) 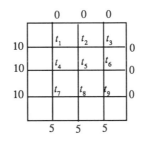   (iii)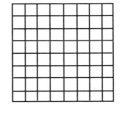

and applying the result that:

'at each interior point of the mesh, the temperature is the average of the temperatures at the four neighbouring points'

Thus in (i), $t_1 = \frac{1}{4}(0 + 0 + 5 + 10) = 3.75$

2. (a) In figure (ii) express t_1 in terms of t_2 and t_4

    (b) Write down 8 other similar equations, but do not solve them!

3. Explain why the mesh in (iii) would give a more accurate answer. What would be the disadvantage in taking a mesh of this size?

Triangular matrices

1. (a) For $L = \begin{bmatrix} 1 & 0 & 0 \\ 3 & 1 & 0 \\ 2 & 4 & 1 \end{bmatrix}$ and $b = \begin{bmatrix} 2 \\ 10 \\ 17 \end{bmatrix}$, solve $L\,y = b$.

   [L is called a lower triangular matrix]

   (b) For $U = \begin{bmatrix} 4 & -2 & 6 \\ 0 & 5 & 1 \\ 0 & 0 & 3 \end{bmatrix}$, solve $U\,x = y$

   [U is called an upper triangular matrix]

   (c) Find the matrix product $A = LU$

   (d) Explain why x is the solution of $Ax = b$.

2. You can express a general square matrix as a product LU, where L is a lower triangular matrix with 1's on its diagonal and U is an upper triangular matrix.

   (a) Solve $\begin{bmatrix} 5 & -3 & 2 \\ 10 & -4 & 3 \\ 20 & -16 & 13 \end{bmatrix} = \begin{bmatrix} 1 & 0 & 0 \\ l & 1 & 0 \\ m & n & 1 \end{bmatrix} \begin{bmatrix} r & s & t \\ 0 & u & v \\ 0 & 0 & w \end{bmatrix}$

   (b) Describe a good order in which to find the unknown coefficients.

3. Use LU decomposition to solve the equation

$$\begin{bmatrix} 2 & -3 & 1 \\ 1 & -1 & 2 \\ 4 & 0 & 1 \end{bmatrix} \begin{bmatrix} x_1 \\ x_2 \\ x_3 \end{bmatrix} = \begin{bmatrix} 0 \\ -1 \\ 7 \end{bmatrix}$$

Gauss Seidel

1.   (a)   Sketch the graphs of the simultaneous equations:

$$6x + 2y = 3 \quad ① \quad \text{and} \quad 2x - 6y = 19 \quad ②$$

     (b)   Estimate the values of x and y correct to the nearest integer.

The Gauss Seidel method involves rearranging these equations as shown:

From ① $x = \dfrac{3 - 2y}{6}$

From ②, $y = \dfrac{2x - 19}{6}$

By analogy with the iterative method for solving equations in a single variable, these equations give rise to two iterative formulas:

$$x_{n+1} = \frac{3 - 2y_n}{6} \quad \text{and} \quad y_{n+1} = \frac{2x_{n+1} - 19}{6}$$

Note that x_{n+1} has to be expressed in terms of y_n, the value of y from the **previous** iteration, whilst y_{n+1} can be expressed in terms of x_{n+1}, the value that has just been calculated.

2.   (a)   Take the values that you chose in question 1(b) as x_0, y_0 and use the iterative formulas to find x_n, y_n for $n = 1, 2, 3, 4$.

     (b)   On your sketch of the graphs, mark and join the points (x_0, y_0), (x_1, y_0), (x_1, y_1), (x_2, y_1) which correspond to successive iterations. What do you notice?

     (c)   For what starting values (x_0, y_0) does the iteration converge?

     (d)   Use the ideas above to find a pair of equations for which the Gauss Seidel iteration does **not** converge.

3.   Use the Gauss Seidel method to solve the equations

$$8x - 3y = 5 \quad \text{and} \quad 2x + 7y = 11$$

4.   Explain how you would generalise the Gauss Seidel method to solve equations in more than two unknowns.

Using computer packages

1. (a) Use a program to solve the following equations by Gaussian elimination. (A suitable BBC BASIC program is given in the *Unit Guide*).

$$50x_1 + x_2 + 2x_3 = 5$$

$$x_1 + 16x_2 + 2x_3 = 11$$

$$x_1 \qquad + 13x_3 = 2$$

(b) Use the same program to solve the equations in the order:

$$x_1 \qquad + 13x_3 = 2$$

$$50x_1 + x_2 + 2x_3 = 5$$

$$x_1 + 16x_2 + 2x_3 = 11$$

(c) Your solutions in (a) and (b) will not be precisely the same. Compare your two solutions by evaluating the expressions $50x_1 + x_2 + 2x_3 - 5$, $x_1 + 16x_2 + 2x_3 - 11$ and $x_1 + 13x_3 - 2$. [These expressions, which should be zero for exact solutions, are known as residuals].

Which order for the equations appears to be best?

2. On Tasksheet 1 you obtained the following equations for the temperature distribution in a square plate.

$$t_1 = \tfrac{1}{4}(10 + 0 + t_2 + t_4) \qquad\qquad t_6 = \tfrac{1}{4}(t_5 + t_3 + 0 + t_9)$$

$$t_2 = \tfrac{1}{4}(t_1 + 0 + t_3 + t_5) \qquad\qquad t_7 = \tfrac{1}{4}(10 + t_4 + t_8 + 5)$$

$$t_3 = \tfrac{1}{4}(t_2 + 0 + 0 + t_6) \qquad\qquad t_8 = \tfrac{1}{4}(t_7 + t_5 + t_9 + 5)$$

$$t_4 = \tfrac{1}{4}(10 + t_1 + t_5 + t_7) \qquad\qquad t_9 = \tfrac{1}{4}(t_8 + t_6 + 0 + 5)$$

$$t_5 = \tfrac{1}{4}(t_4 + t_2 + t_6 + t_8)$$

Use a Gaussian elimination program to solve these equations once they have been put into the standard form:

$$4t_1 - t_2 - 0t_3 - t_4 - 0t_5 - 0t_6 - 0t_7 - 0t_8 - 0t_9 = 10$$
etc.

(continued)

98

In carrying out Gaussian elimination it is best to arrange the equations so that the pivot is the largest possible coefficient at each stage. For example, at a stage such as:

x_1	x_2	x_3	c	
4.3	9.7	1.8	3.4	①
0	3.1	7.2	7.5	②
0	5.9	1.3	8.1	③

it would be (marginally) better to interchange rows ② and ③. A simple rule of thumb is to arrange the equations initially so that they have a **strong leading diagonal** i.e. so that the coefficients of x_1 in equation ①, x_2 in ② and x_3 in ③ are relatively large.

3. It is easy to write your own program for Gauss Seidel iteration. A BBC BASIC program and a program for the fx 7000G calculator are given in the *Unit Guide*. Use such a program to solve the following equations in the orders given.

(a) $50x + y + 2z = 5$
$x + 16y + 2z = 11$
$x + 13z = 2$

(b) $x + 13z = 2$
$50x + y + 2z = 5$
$x + 16y + 2z = 11$

For Gauss Seidel iteration it is better to arrange the equations so that they have a strong leading diagonal.

> **Convergence of the Gauss Seidel method is difficult to predict. However, convergence is guaranteed if, for each row, the element on the diagonal is greater than the sum of the remaining elements:**
>
> $$\left| a_{ii} \right| > \sum_{i \neq j} a_{ij}$$

4. (a) Use a suitable program to perform 4 iterations with starting values $x_0 = y_0 = z_0 = 0$ for the set of equations:

$$5x - 2y + 4z = 2$$
$$2x + 8y - 6z = 5$$
$$x - 2y + 5z = 8$$

(b) To indicate the accuracy of the values x_4, y_4, z_4 as solutions for the equations, evaluate the residual

$$5x_4 - 2y_4 + 4z_4 - 2$$

and the residuals for the other two equations.

Ill conditioning

1.   (a)   Solve the simultaneous equations:

(i) $y = 1.50x + 1.00$

$y = 1.51x + 2.00$

(ii) $y = 1.50x + 1.00$

$y = 1.49x + 2.00$

What do you notice about the solutions?

(b)   Sketch the graph of $y = 1.50x + 1.00$. On the same diagram, sketch the graphs of $y = 1.51x + 2.00$ and $y = 1.49x + 2.00$

(c)   Use your graphs to explain why there is such a large difference in the answers to the two sets of equations, despite the very small differences in the coefficients.

2.   (a)   Solve the equations

$$x - 11y = 1$$

$$-9x + 100y = 1$$

(b)   Solve the equations

$$x - 11y = 1$$

$$-9x + 98y = 1$$

(c)   A 2% change in the coefficient of y has caused a huge change in the solution. Sketch the graphs of $x - 11y = 1$, $-9x + 100y = 1$ and $-9x + 98y = 1$ on the same axes and explain what is happening

Equations where small changes in the coefficients lead to large changes in the solution are known as **ill conditioned**. If the coefficients in the equations in question 1 had been rounded to one decimal place they would have given the equations:

$$y = 1.5x + 1.0$$

$$y = 1.5x + 2.0$$

which have no solution! Not all ill conditioned equations are so obvious and if the coefficients have been rounded before the equation is solved then the final result may well have such a huge error associated with it as to be meaningless.

3.   Invent a pair of ill conditioned equations.

Tutorial sheet

1. Rearrange the set of equations:

$$2x + 9y - 3z = 5$$
$$4x + y + 7z = 9$$
$$9x + 2y - z = 11$$

and solve

(a) using Gaussian elimination;

(b) using the Gauss Seidel method;

(c) using **LU** decomposition.

2. Which method would you use to solve each of the following sets of equations, and why? (There is no need to solve them!)

(a) $3x_1 + 7x_2 - 8x_3 = 2$
   $5x_1 - 2x_2 + 9x_3 = 6$
   $2x_1 + 5x_2 - x_3 = 10$

(b) $5x_1 + 3x_2 - x_3 + 5x_4 = 2$
   $6x_2 + 3x_3 - 7x_4 = 5$
   $6x_3 + 9x_4 = -7$
   $11x_4 = 14$

(c) Several sets of 10 x 10 equations of the form $\mathbf{Ax} = \mathbf{b}$ with a fixed $\mathbf{A}$, but various $\mathbf{b}$'s.

3. How would you use the methods given in the chapter to find $\mathbf{A}^{-1}$ for any n x n matrix $\mathbf{A}$?

4. The equations $2.4x - 3.7y = 5$ ① $6.2x - 9.6y = 3$ ②

have had the coefficients of x and y rounded to 1 decimal place.

(a) (i) What are the greatest possible and least possible gradients of line ① ?

(ii) What are the greatest possible and least possible gradients of line ② ?

(b) By taking the greatest gradient of ① and the least gradient of ②, find a possible solution to the equations.

(c) By taking the least gradient of ① and the greatest gradient of ②, find another possible solution to the equations.

(d) What can you conclude about the solution of the original equations?

6 *Canonical form*

6.1 Kernels

In an earlier chapter you considered the solution of equations involving crushing transformations, such as

$$\begin{bmatrix} 2 & 3 \\ 2 & 3 \end{bmatrix}\begin{bmatrix} x \\ y \end{bmatrix} = \begin{bmatrix} 5 \\ 5 \end{bmatrix}$$

(a) **Find the general solution of**

$$\begin{bmatrix} 2 & 3 \\ 2 & 3 \end{bmatrix}\begin{bmatrix} x \\ y \end{bmatrix} = \begin{bmatrix} 0 \\ 0 \end{bmatrix}.$$

(b) **Find a particular solution of**

$$\begin{bmatrix} 2 & 3 \\ 2 & 3 \end{bmatrix}\begin{bmatrix} x \\ y \end{bmatrix} = \begin{bmatrix} 5 \\ 5 \end{bmatrix}.$$

(c) **Find the general solution of**

$$\begin{bmatrix} 2 & 3 \\ 2 & 3 \end{bmatrix}\begin{bmatrix} x \\ y \end{bmatrix} = \begin{bmatrix} 5 \\ 5 \end{bmatrix}.$$

(d) **What is the connection between your answers to parts (a), (b) and (c)? Does this result generalise?**

The set of vectors transformed to $\mathbf{0}$ by a matrix $\mathbf{A}$ is called the **kernel** of the matrix, Ker ($\mathbf{A}$). The kernel of a matrix always contains $\mathbf{0}$ because $\mathbf{A0} = \mathbf{0}$ for any matrix $\mathbf{A}$. Furthermore, if the kernel contains a non-zero vector, then it contains any multiple of that vector:

$$\mathbf{k} \in \text{Ker}\,(\mathbf{A}) \implies \lambda\,\mathbf{k} \in \text{Ker}\,(\mathbf{A}).$$

This final chapter of the unit is concerned with the insights into simultaneous equations given by an algebraic treatment of matrix equations. The importance of the kernel stems from its connection with the general solution of such equations.

> **If a matrix equation**
> $$\mathbf{Ar} = \mathbf{b}$$
> **has two solutions, $\mathbf{r}_1$ and $\mathbf{r}_2$, then show that**
> $$\mathbf{r}_2 = \mathbf{r}_1 + \mathbf{k}, \quad \mathbf{k} \in \text{Ker}\,(\mathbf{A}).$$

Conversely, if $\mathbf{p}$ is any particular solution of $\mathbf{Ar} = \mathbf{b}$ and $\mathbf{k}$ is any element of Ker ($\mathbf{A}$), then

$$\mathbf{A}\,(\mathbf{p} + \mathbf{k}) = \mathbf{Ap} + \mathbf{Ak} = \mathbf{b} + \mathbf{0} = \mathbf{b}$$

and so $\mathbf{p} + \mathbf{k}$ is also a solution.

For example, the general solution of

$$\begin{bmatrix} 2 & 3 \\ 2 & 3 \end{bmatrix} \begin{bmatrix} x \\ y \end{bmatrix} = \begin{bmatrix} 5 \\ 5 \end{bmatrix}$$

is of the form

$$\begin{bmatrix} x \\ y \end{bmatrix} = \begin{bmatrix} 1 \\ 1 \end{bmatrix} + \lambda \begin{bmatrix} -3 \\ 2 \end{bmatrix},$$

where $\begin{bmatrix} 1 \\ 1 \end{bmatrix}$ could be replaced by **any** other particular solution, for example $\begin{bmatrix} -2 \\ 3 \end{bmatrix}$.

Example 1

Find the general solution of

$$\begin{bmatrix} 4 & 1 & 3 \\ -8 & -1 & -13 \end{bmatrix} \begin{bmatrix} x \\ y \\ z \end{bmatrix} = \begin{bmatrix} 2 \\ -2 \end{bmatrix}$$

Solution

It is easy to spot the particular solution $\begin{bmatrix} 0 \\ 2 \\ 0 \end{bmatrix}$.

The kernel can be found by solving

$$4x + y + 3z = 0 \qquad ①$$

$$-8x - y - 13z = 0 \qquad ②$$

$$① + ②, \quad -4x - 10z = 0$$

$$2① + ②, \quad y - 7z = 0$$

If $z = 2\lambda$, then $x = -5\lambda$ and $y = 14\lambda$. The kernel therefore consists of all vectors of the form $\lambda \begin{bmatrix} -5 \\ 14 \\ 2 \end{bmatrix}$.

The general solution is $\begin{bmatrix} x \\ y \\ z \end{bmatrix} = \begin{bmatrix} 0 \\ 2 \\ 0 \end{bmatrix} + \lambda \begin{bmatrix} -5 \\ 14 \\ 2 \end{bmatrix}.$

6.2   Finding kernels

Canonical form is a general name given to classes of matrices of a simple form. For the purposes of this unit, a matrix will be said to be of canonical form if it has the form

$$\begin{bmatrix} I & * \\ 0 & 0 \end{bmatrix}$$

where **I** is a (square) identity matrix, $*$ is any matrix with the same number of rows as **I** and the **0**'s are matrices consisting entirely of zeros. For example,

$$\left[\begin{array}{cc:ccc} 1 & 0 & 3 & -1 & 1 \\ 0 & 1 & 1 & 0 & 2 \\ \hdashline 0 & 0 & 0 & 0 & 0 \end{array}\right]$$

One important feature of this form is that it is easy to find the kernel and solve equations for a matrix in canonical form.

Example 2

Find the kernel of $\begin{bmatrix} 1 & 0 & 3 & -1 & 1 \\ 0 & 1 & 1 & 0 & 2 \\ 0 & 0 & 0 & 0 & 0 \end{bmatrix}$

Solution

$$\begin{bmatrix} 1 & 0 & 3 & -1 & 1 \\ 0 & 1 & 1 & 0 & 2 \\ 0 & 0 & 0 & 0 & 0 \end{bmatrix}\begin{bmatrix} x \\ y \\ z \\ t \\ u \end{bmatrix} = \begin{bmatrix} 0 \\ 0 \\ 0 \end{bmatrix} \Rightarrow \begin{cases} x = -3z + t - u \\ y = -z - 2u \end{cases}$$

Let $z = \lambda$, $t = \mu$, $u = \gamma$. Then

$$\begin{bmatrix} x \\ y \\ z \\ t \\ u \end{bmatrix} = \lambda\begin{bmatrix} -3 \\ -1 \\ 1 \\ 0 \\ 0 \end{bmatrix} + \mu\begin{bmatrix} 1 \\ 0 \\ 0 \\ 1 \\ 0 \end{bmatrix} + \gamma\begin{bmatrix} -1 \\ -2 \\ 0 \\ 0 \\ 1 \end{bmatrix}; \quad \lambda,\ \mu\ \gamma \in \mathbb{R}$$

It is possible to simply write down the kernel for a matrix in canonical form. This is investigated on Tasksheet 1.

 TASKSHEET 1 - *Kernels*

Other important features of canonical form are that

*   it is reasonably easy to reduce matrices to this form by using row operations;

*   the kernel of the reduced matrix is the same as that of the original matrix.

Example 3

Use row operations to reduce the matrix $\begin{bmatrix} 2 & -1 & 2 \\ 1 & -3 & 3 \\ 3 & 1 & 1 \end{bmatrix}$ to canonical form. Hence find the kernel of this matrix.

Solution

Denoting the rows of the matrix by ①, ② and ③ :

$$
\begin{array}{ll}
① & \\
2② - ① & \begin{bmatrix} 2 & -1 & 2 \\ 0 & -5 & 4 \\ 0 & 5 & -4 \end{bmatrix} \qquad \begin{array}{l} ① \\ ④ \\ ⑤ \end{array}
\end{array}
$$

$$
\begin{array}{ll}
\frac{1}{2}① & \\
-\frac{1}{5}④ & \begin{bmatrix} 1 & -\frac{1}{2} & 1 \\ 0 & 1 & -\frac{4}{5} \\ 0 & 0 & 0 \end{bmatrix} \qquad \begin{array}{l} ⑥ \\ ⑦ \\ ⑧ \end{array}
\end{array}
$$

$$
\begin{array}{ll}
⑥ + \frac{1}{2}⑦ & \\
⑦ & \left[\begin{array}{cc|c} 1 & 0 & \frac{3}{5} \\ 0 & 1 & -\frac{4}{5} \\ \hline 0 & 0 & 0 \end{array} \right]
\end{array}
$$

The kernel consists of all vectors of the form $\lambda \begin{bmatrix} -\frac{3}{5} \\ \frac{4}{5} \\ 1 \end{bmatrix}$. This form can be written more neatly as $\mu \begin{bmatrix} -3 \\ 4 \\ 5 \end{bmatrix}$.

If a kernel contains non-zero vectors then the transformation is a crushing transformation and dimensions are lost in the transformation. In the above example, the line

$$
\begin{bmatrix} x \\ y \\ z \end{bmatrix} = \mu \begin{bmatrix} -3 \\ 4 \\ 5 \end{bmatrix}
$$

is crushed onto the orgin and so 1 dimension is lost in the transformation.

Exercise 1

1. Reduce each of the following matrices to canonical form and hence state the kernel for each of them.

   (a) $\begin{bmatrix} 4 & -2 & 2 \\ -1 & 4 & -3 \\ 5 & 8 & -5 \end{bmatrix}$

   (b) $\begin{bmatrix} 3 & -4 & 2 \\ 5 & 1 & 2 \\ 7 & 6 & 2 \end{bmatrix}$

   (c) $\begin{bmatrix} 1 & 0 & 3 \\ 4 & -1 & 2 \\ -2 & 1 & 0 \end{bmatrix}$

2. Find the kernel for

   $$\begin{bmatrix} 2 & -1 & 0 & 1 \\ 1 & 0 & -3 & 4 \\ 3 & -2 & 3 & -2 \\ -1 & -1 & 9 & -11 \end{bmatrix}$$

3. The matrix S is given by

   $$S = \begin{bmatrix} -1 & 3 & 1 & 0 & 3 \\ 2 & -2 & 0 & 1 & 2 \\ 1 & 5 & 3 & 2 & 13 \\ 7 & -13 & -3 & 2 & -5 \end{bmatrix}$$

   (a) Find the kernel for S.

   (b) How many dimensions are lost in applying the transformation S ?

6.3   General solutions

You have seen how to use row operations to express a matrix in canonical form in order to find the kernel. This method can be extended to find particular solutions and hence the general solution. For example, suppose you need to find the general solution for

$$x - 2y + z = 5$$

$$2x + y + 4z = 9$$

$$3x - y + 5z = 14$$

You can first reduce the matrix $\begin{bmatrix} 1 & -2 & 1 & 5 \\ 2 & 1 & 4 & 9 \\ 3 & -1 & 5 & 14 \end{bmatrix}$ to its canonical form, $\begin{bmatrix} 1 & 0 & \frac{9}{5} & \frac{23}{5} \\ 0 & 1 & \frac{2}{5} & -\frac{1}{5} \\ 0 & 0 & 0 & 0 \end{bmatrix}$

> **Check the above assertion.**

This means that row operations can be applied to the original equations to give the equations

$$\begin{bmatrix} 1 & 0 & \frac{9}{5} \\ 0 & 1 & \frac{2}{5} \\ 0 & 0 & 0 \end{bmatrix} \begin{bmatrix} x \\ y \\ z \end{bmatrix} = \begin{bmatrix} \frac{23}{5} \\ -\frac{1}{5} \\ 0 \end{bmatrix}$$

From this form, both a particular solution and the kernel can be written down on inspection.

The general solution is $\begin{bmatrix} x \\ y \\ z \end{bmatrix} = \begin{bmatrix} \frac{23}{5} \\ -\frac{1}{5} \\ 0 \end{bmatrix} + \lambda \begin{bmatrix} -9 \\ -2 \\ 5 \end{bmatrix}$

The above example illustrates the general method for solving any matrix equation $\mathbf{Ar} = \mathbf{b}$.

- Reduce the matrix $[\mathbf{A} \mid \mathbf{b}]$ to canonical form

$$\begin{bmatrix} \mathbf{I} & \mathbf{k}_1 & \mathbf{k}_2 & \cdots & \mathbf{p} \\ \mathbf{0} & \mathbf{0} & \mathbf{0} & \cdots & \mathbf{q} \end{bmatrix}$$

- If $\mathbf{q} \neq \mathbf{0}$, then the equations have no solution.

- If $\mathbf{q} = \mathbf{0}$, $\quad \mathbf{r} = \begin{bmatrix} \mathbf{p} \\ 0 \\ 0 \\ 0 \\ \vdots \end{bmatrix} + \lambda \begin{bmatrix} -\mathbf{k}_1 \\ 1 \\ 0 \\ 0 \\ \vdots \end{bmatrix} + \mu \begin{bmatrix} -\mathbf{k}_2 \\ 0 \\ 1 \\ 0 \\ \vdots \end{bmatrix} + \cdots$

Previously you have seen that there are three possibilities for simultaneous equations:

- no solutions;
- a unique solution;
- infinitely many solutions.

These correspond to the three matrix algebra possibilities:

- no particular solution exists;
- a particular solution exists and the kernel consists only of $\mathbf{0}$;
- a particular solution exists and the kernel contains a non-zero vector (and hence contains infinitely many vectors).

The three possibilities for matrix equations are illustrated in the table:

Canonical form	Solution
$\left[\begin{array}{ccc\|c} 1 & 0 & 3 & 2 \\ 0 & 1 & 1 & 1 \\ 0 & 0 & 0 & 1 \end{array}\right]$	No solution
$\left[\begin{array}{cc\|c} 1 & 0 & 2 \\ 0 & 1 & 1 \\ 0 & 0 & 0 \end{array}\right]$	Unique solution $\left[\begin{array}{c} 2 \\ 1 \end{array}\right]$
$\left[\begin{array}{ccc\|c} 1 & 0 & 3 & 2 \\ 0 & 1 & 1 & 1 \\ 0 & 0 & 0 & 0 \end{array}\right]$	Solutions $\left[\begin{array}{c} 2 \\ 1 \\ 0 \end{array}\right] + \lambda \left[\begin{array}{c} -3 \\ -1 \\ 1 \end{array}\right]$

Exercise 2

1. Solve, using appropriate methods

(a) $\begin{aligned} x + 3y &= 5 \\ -2x + 5y &= 1 \\ 4x - 3y &= 5 \end{aligned}$

(b) $\begin{aligned} 3x + 4y - z &= 9 \\ x + 3y + 3z &= 8 \\ 3x - y - 11z &= -6 \end{aligned}$

(c) $\begin{aligned} x + 4y - 3z + s + t &= -7 \\ 2x - y + z + 4s + t &= 0 \end{aligned}$

2. The transformation T is given by the matrix

$$T = \begin{bmatrix} 1 & -1 & 0 & 1 \\ 5 & 2 & -4 & 1 \\ 2 & 5 & -4 & -2 \\ 9 & 5 & -8 & 1 \end{bmatrix}$$

(a) What is the kernel of the transformation?

(b) What is crushed onto the point with position vector $\begin{bmatrix} 5 \\ 4 \\ -11 \\ 3 \end{bmatrix}$?

After working through this chapter you should:

1. be able to find the kernel of a matrix;

2. be able to find particular solutions and the general solution of a set of linear equations;

3. know how to reduce a matrix to canonical form;

4. know how to write down particular solutions and the kernel from canonical form.

Kernels

You have seen that the kernel of the matrix

$$\begin{bmatrix} 1 & 0 & 3 & -1 & 1 \\ 0 & 1 & 1 & 0 & 2 \\ 0 & 0 & 0 & 0 & 0 \end{bmatrix}$$

consists of all the vectors of the form

$$\lambda \begin{bmatrix} -3 \\ -1 \\ 1 \\ 0 \\ 0 \end{bmatrix} + \mu \begin{bmatrix} 1 \\ 0 \\ 0 \\ 1 \\ 0 \end{bmatrix} + \gamma \begin{bmatrix} -1 \\ 2 \\ 0 \\ 0 \\ 1 \end{bmatrix}$$

1.　(a)　Find the kernel for the matrix transformation

$$\begin{bmatrix} 1 & 0 & 0 & 1 & 2 \\ 0 & 1 & 0 & -2 & 0 \\ 0 & 0 & 1 & -1 & -1 \\ 0 & 0 & 0 & 0 & 0 \end{bmatrix}$$

in the same form as the kernel given above.

　(b)　What connection can you see between the elements in the canonical form matrix and the elements in the vectors of the kernel?

2.　(a)　Check your conjecture in 1(b) with another canonical form matrix of your own choosing.

　(b)　Justify your conjecture as rigorously as you can.

Tutorial sheet

1. (a) Reduce the matrix

$$\begin{bmatrix} 1 & -2 & 1 & 1 \\ 3 & -1 & 6 & 1 \\ 1 & 3 & 4 & 3 \end{bmatrix}$$

to canonical form.

   (b) Hence solve

$$x - 2y + z = 1$$

$$3x - y + 6z = 1$$

$$x + 3y + 4z = 3$$

2. (a) Reduce the matrix

$$\begin{bmatrix} 1 & -2 & 1 & 1 \\ 3 & -1 & 5 & 1 \\ 1 & 3 & 4 & 3 \end{bmatrix}$$

to canonical form

   (b) Hence solve

$$x - 2y + z = 1$$

$$3x - y + 5z = 1$$

$$x + 3y + 4z = 3$$

3. For the simultaneous equations

$$3x + 5y = 1$$

$$-2x + y + 4z = 3$$

$$5x + 17y + 8z = t$$

   (a) Use canonical form to find the kernel.

   (b) For what value of t are the equations consistent?

   (c) Find the general solution for the consistent set of equations.

1 Introduction to matrices

1.1 Data storage

An hour's sales of soft drinks at one cash till are given by the matrix

$$B = \begin{bmatrix} 9 & 12 & 11 \\ 3 & 7 & 2 \end{bmatrix}$$

(a) How many medium colas were sold?

(b) What information is given by the element b_{21}?

(c) Evalute $\displaystyle\sum_{i=1}^{2} \sum_{j=1}^{3} b_{ij}$

What information does this represent?

(a) 12

(b) b_{21} is the element in the 2nd row and 1st column. Thus it represents the number of small root beers that were sold.

(c) $$\sum_{i=1}^{2} \sum_{j=1}^{3} b_{ij} = \sum_{i=1}^{2} (b_{i1} + b_{i2} + b_{i3})$$

$$= (b_{11} + b_{12} + b_{13}) + (b_{21} + b_{22} + b_{23})$$

It represents the sum of all the elements of the matrix or the total number of soft drinks sold at one cash till in one hour.

1.2 Matrix arithmetic

Exercise 1

1. (a) $\begin{bmatrix} 1 & 2 \\ 3 & 12 \end{bmatrix}$ (b) $\begin{bmatrix} 7 & 11 \\ -6 & 2 \\ 4 & -8 \end{bmatrix}$ (c) $\begin{bmatrix} 28 & -14 \\ 21 & 63 \end{bmatrix}$ (d) $\begin{bmatrix} \frac{7}{5} & \frac{1}{5} & \frac{8}{5} \\ \frac{12}{5} & -2 & \frac{4}{5} \end{bmatrix}$

(e) $\begin{bmatrix} -12 & 10 \\ -9 & 39 \end{bmatrix}$ (f) $\begin{bmatrix} 110 & -78 & 16 \\ 6 & -46 & 64 \\ 9 & 13 & -28 \end{bmatrix}$ (g) $\begin{bmatrix} 27 & 75 \\ 64 & 28 \end{bmatrix}$

2. (a) (i) $\begin{bmatrix} 0.2 & 0.1 \\ 0.4 & 0.5 \\ 0.4 & 0.4 \end{bmatrix}$ (ii) $\begin{bmatrix} 0.3 & 0.5 & 0 \\ 0.3 & 0 & 0.8 \\ 0.4 & 0.5 & 0.2 \end{bmatrix}$

(b) $\begin{bmatrix} 6 \\ 18 \\ 16 \end{bmatrix}$ (c) $\begin{bmatrix} 0.3 & 0.5 & 0 \\ 0.3 & 0 & 0.8 \\ 0.4 & 0.5 & 0.2 \end{bmatrix} \begin{bmatrix} 6 \\ 18 \\ 16 \end{bmatrix} = \begin{bmatrix} 10.8 \\ 14.6 \\ 14.6 \end{bmatrix}$

(d) $\begin{bmatrix} 0.3 & 0.5 & 0 \\ 0.3 & 0 & 0.8 \\ 0.4 & 0.5 & 0.2 \end{bmatrix} \begin{bmatrix} 0.2 & 0.1 \\ 0.4 & 0.5 \\ 0.4 & 0.4 \end{bmatrix} = \begin{bmatrix} 0.26 & 0.28 \\ 0.38 & 0.35 \\ 0.36 & 0.37 \end{bmatrix}$

(e) $\begin{bmatrix} 0.26 & 0.28 \\ 0.38 & 0.35 \\ 0.36 & 0.37 \end{bmatrix} \begin{bmatrix} 20 \\ 20 \end{bmatrix} = \begin{bmatrix} 10.8 \\ 14.6 \\ 14.6 \end{bmatrix}$

1.3 Properties of matrix arithmetic

Exercise 2

1. (a) Cannot be carried out.

(b) Cannot be carried out.

(c) 2 x 4

(d) 3 x 2

(e) Cannot be carried out.

(f) 1 x 2

(g) Cannot be carried out.

2. (a) (i) $\begin{bmatrix} 1 & a \\ 0 & 1 \end{bmatrix}\begin{bmatrix} 1 & b \\ 0 & 1 \end{bmatrix} = \begin{bmatrix} 1 & a+b \\ 0 & 1 \end{bmatrix} = \begin{bmatrix} 1 & c \\ 0 & 1 \end{bmatrix}$. Closed

(ii) $\begin{bmatrix} 1 & 2 \\ 2 & 1 \end{bmatrix}\begin{bmatrix} 1 & 3 \\ 3 & 1 \end{bmatrix} = \begin{bmatrix} 7 & 5 \\ 5 & 7 \end{bmatrix}$. Not closed

(iii) $\begin{bmatrix} a & b \\ 0 & a \end{bmatrix}\begin{bmatrix} c & d \\ 0 & c \end{bmatrix} = \begin{bmatrix} ac & ad+bc \\ 0 & ac \end{bmatrix} = \begin{bmatrix} e & f \\ 0 & e \end{bmatrix}$. Closed

(b) (i) $\begin{bmatrix} 1 & b \\ 0 & 1 \end{bmatrix}\begin{bmatrix} 1 & a \\ 0 & 1 \end{bmatrix} = \begin{bmatrix} 1 & b+a \\ 0 & 1 \end{bmatrix}$. Commutative

(ii) $\begin{bmatrix} 1 & a \\ a & 1 \end{bmatrix}\begin{bmatrix} 1 & b \\ b & 1 \end{bmatrix} = \begin{bmatrix} 1+ab & b+a \\ a+b & ab+1 \end{bmatrix}$

$\begin{bmatrix} 1 & b \\ b & 1 \end{bmatrix}\begin{bmatrix} 1 & a \\ a & 1 \end{bmatrix} = \begin{bmatrix} 1+ba & a+b \\ b+a & ba+1 \end{bmatrix}$. Commutative

(iii) $\begin{bmatrix} c & d \\ 0 & c \end{bmatrix}\begin{bmatrix} a & b \\ 0 & a \end{bmatrix} = \begin{bmatrix} ac & cb+da \\ 0 & ca \end{bmatrix}$. Commutative

1.4 Transition matrices

(a) Explain why the output matrix after the first stage of the process is given by Ta.

(b) What is the output matrix after the second stage in terms of T and a?

(c) What is the output matrix after the third stage in terms of T and a?

(d) If the process were to have n stages instead of three, what would be the output at the final stage?

(a) The output at A, $\quad a = \dfrac{1}{3} \times 100 + \dfrac{1}{4} \times 200$

the output at B, $\quad b = \dfrac{2}{3} \times 100 + \dfrac{3}{4} \times 200$

$\Rightarrow \quad \begin{bmatrix} a \\ b \end{bmatrix} = \begin{bmatrix} \frac{1}{3} & \frac{1}{4} \\ \frac{2}{3} & \frac{3}{4} \end{bmatrix}\begin{bmatrix} 100 \\ 200 \end{bmatrix} = Ta$

(b)   For outputs c and d, $\begin{bmatrix} c \\ d \end{bmatrix} = \mathbf{T} \begin{bmatrix} a \\ b \end{bmatrix} = \mathbf{T}(\mathbf{T}\mathbf{a}) = \mathbf{T}^2\mathbf{a}$

(c)   Similarly, for outputs e and f, $\begin{bmatrix} e \\ f \end{bmatrix} = \mathbf{T} \begin{bmatrix} c \\ d \end{bmatrix} = \mathbf{T}(\mathbf{T}^2\mathbf{a}) = \mathbf{T}^3\mathbf{a}$

(d)   Generalising this result gives $\mathbf{T}^n\mathbf{a}$ as the output after the n th stage.

Exercise 3

1.   (a)

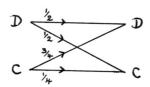

   (b) $\mathbf{a}_1 = \begin{bmatrix} 0 \\ 1 \end{bmatrix}$ $\mathbf{a}_2 = \begin{bmatrix} \frac{3}{4} \\ \frac{1}{4} \end{bmatrix}$

   (c) $\mathbf{T} = \begin{bmatrix} \frac{1}{2} & \frac{3}{4} \\ \frac{1}{2} & \frac{1}{4} \end{bmatrix}$ (d) $\mathbf{a}_n = \mathbf{T}^{n-1}\,\mathbf{a}_1$

2.

   (a) $\begin{array}{cc} & \begin{array}{cc} F & B \end{array} \\ \begin{array}{c} F \\ B \end{array} & \begin{bmatrix} \frac{1}{5} & \frac{1}{3} \\ \frac{4}{5} & \frac{2}{3} \end{bmatrix} \end{array} = \mathbf{T}$

   (b) $\mathbf{T}^2 \begin{bmatrix} 0 \\ 1 \end{bmatrix} = \begin{bmatrix} \frac{13}{45} \\ \frac{32}{45} \end{bmatrix}$ Probability $\frac{32}{45}$

   (c) $\mathbf{T}^3 = \begin{bmatrix} 0.29 & 0.30 \\ 0.71 & 0.70 \end{bmatrix}$

        (i) $\mathbf{T}^3 \begin{bmatrix} 0 \\ 1 \end{bmatrix} = \begin{bmatrix} 0.30 \\ 0.70 \end{bmatrix}$ (ii) $\mathbf{T}^3 \begin{bmatrix} 1 \\ 0 \end{bmatrix} = \begin{bmatrix} 0.29 \\ 0.71 \end{bmatrix}$

        Probability 0.70   Probability 0.71

3. $\begin{array}{cc} & \begin{array}{cc} F & W \end{array} \\ \mathbf{T} = \begin{array}{c} F \\ W \end{array} & \begin{bmatrix} \frac{4}{5} & \frac{2}{3} \\ \frac{1}{5} & \frac{1}{3} \end{bmatrix} \end{array}$ $\mathbf{T}^2 \begin{bmatrix} 1 \\ 0 \end{bmatrix} = \begin{bmatrix} \frac{58}{75} \\ \frac{17}{75} \end{bmatrix}$

                        Probability $\frac{58}{75}$

2 Matrices and transformations

2.1 Transformations

> (a) Give examples, from the diagram, of a 90° rotation, a reflection and a translation.
>
> (b) What is the image of F_1 when it is rotated 180° about the origin?

(a) **90° rotations** (anticlockwise)

$F_7 \rightarrow F_8$ centre $(7.5, 1.5)$

$F_4 \rightarrow F_3$ centre $(0, 0)$

$F_6 \rightarrow F_3$ centre $(-2.5, 0.5)$

$F_3 \rightarrow F_1$ centre $(0, 0)$

$F_8 \rightarrow F_5$ centre $(9, -3)$

$F_8 \rightarrow F_9$ centre $(2, -4)$

$F_8 \rightarrow F_2$ centre $(2.5, -6.5)$

Reflections

$F_1 \leftrightarrow F_7$ mirror line $x = 1$ $\qquad$ $F_1 \leftrightarrow F_2$ reflection in $y = 0$

$F_2 \leftrightarrow F_4$ mirror line $x = 0$ $\qquad$ $F_2 \leftrightarrow F_3$ reflection $x + y = 0$

Translations

$F_2 \rightarrow F_5$ shift vector $\begin{bmatrix} 10 \\ -3 \end{bmatrix}$ $\qquad$ $F_9 \rightarrow F_5$ shift vector $\begin{bmatrix} 8 \\ -6 \end{bmatrix}$

$F_5 \rightarrow F_2$ shift vector $\begin{bmatrix} -10 \\ 3 \end{bmatrix}$ $\qquad$ $F_5 \rightarrow F_9$ shift vector $\begin{bmatrix} -8 \\ 6 \end{bmatrix}$

$F_2 \rightarrow F_9$ shift vector $\begin{bmatrix} 2 \\ 3 \end{bmatrix}$ $\qquad$ $F_4 \rightarrow F_6$ shift vector $\begin{bmatrix} -3 \\ -2 \end{bmatrix}$

$F_9 \rightarrow F_2$ shift vector $\begin{bmatrix} -2 \\ -3 \end{bmatrix}$ $\qquad$ $F_6 \rightarrow F_4$ shift vector $\begin{bmatrix} 3 \\ 2 \end{bmatrix}$

(b) The image of F_1 under 180° rotation about $(0, 0)$ is F_4.

Exercise 1

1. (a) $F_1 \rightarrow F_2$ reflection in $y = 0$

    (b) $F_2 \rightarrow F_3$ reflection in $x + y = 0$

    (c) $F_1 \rightarrow F_4$ half turn about $(0, 0)$

    (d) $F_2 \rightarrow F_5$ translation through $\begin{bmatrix} 10 \\ -3 \end{bmatrix}$

    (e) $F_3 \rightarrow F_4$ rotation of $-90°$ (or $+270°$) about $(0, 0)$

    (f) $F_1 \rightarrow F_7$ reflection in $x = 1$.

2. (a) $F_2 \rightarrow F_4$ under a reflection in $x = 0$

    then $F_4 \rightarrow F_3$ under a rotation $90°$ about $(0, 0)$

    $F_2 \rightarrow F_3$ under a reflection in $x + y = 0$

    (b) $F_7 \rightarrow F_1$ under reflection in $x = 1$

    then $F_1 \rightarrow F_2$ under reflection in $y = 0$

    $F_7 \rightarrow F_2$ under rotation $180°$ (centre 1, 0).

3. (a) The inverse is a rotation $90°$ clockwise about $(9, -3)$

    (b) A reflection is always its own inverse.

4. (a) The identity transformation 'has no effect' i.e. it maps any figure onto itself.

    (b) F_6

2.2   Describing transformations

> **Verify that** $\begin{bmatrix} 0 & -1 \\ 1 & 0 \end{bmatrix} \begin{bmatrix} x \\ y \end{bmatrix} = \begin{bmatrix} -y \\ x \end{bmatrix}$

$$\begin{bmatrix} 0 & -1 \\ 1 & 0 \end{bmatrix} \begin{bmatrix} x \\ y \end{bmatrix} = \begin{bmatrix} 0\,x + -1\,y \\ 1\,x + 0\,y \end{bmatrix} = \begin{bmatrix} -y \\ x \end{bmatrix}.$$

2.3 Base vectors

(a) **Express i and j as column vectors.**

(b) **What are the images of i and j when the column vectors are multiplied by the matrices:**

(i) $\begin{bmatrix} 1 & -1 \\ 1 & 1 \end{bmatrix}$, (ii) $\begin{bmatrix} 1 & 3 \\ -1 & 1 \end{bmatrix}$?

(c) **How are the image vectors related to the matrices?**

(a) $\mathbf{i} = \begin{bmatrix} 1 \\ 0 \end{bmatrix}, \quad \mathbf{j} = \begin{bmatrix} 0 \\ 1 \end{bmatrix}$

(b) (i) $\begin{bmatrix} 1 \\ 0 \end{bmatrix} \rightarrow \begin{bmatrix} 1 \\ 1 \end{bmatrix}, \quad \begin{bmatrix} 0 \\ 1 \end{bmatrix} \rightarrow \begin{bmatrix} -1 \\ 1 \end{bmatrix}$

(ii) $\begin{bmatrix} 1 \\ 0 \end{bmatrix} \rightarrow \begin{bmatrix} 1 \\ -1 \end{bmatrix}, \quad \begin{bmatrix} 0 \\ 1 \end{bmatrix} \rightarrow \begin{bmatrix} 3 \\ 1 \end{bmatrix}$

(c) $\begin{bmatrix} 1 \\ 0 \end{bmatrix}$ is mapped onto 'the first column of the matrix'.

$\begin{bmatrix} 0 \\ 1 \end{bmatrix}$ is mapped onto 'the second column of the matrix'.

Work out the matrices for:

(a) **a 60° rotation about the origin,**

(b) **a reflection in the line $y = 2x$.**

(a) The matrix is $\begin{bmatrix} \cos 60 & -\sin 60 \\ \sin 60 & \cos 60 \end{bmatrix} = \begin{bmatrix} \frac{1}{2} & -\frac{\sqrt{3}}{2} \\ \frac{\sqrt{3}}{2} & \frac{1}{2} \end{bmatrix}$

(b)   Tan $\theta = 2$

$\Rightarrow \sin \theta = \dfrac{2}{\sqrt{5}}, \quad \cos \theta = \dfrac{1}{\sqrt{5}}$

$\Rightarrow \cos 2\theta = 2\cos^2 \theta - 1 = \dfrac{-3}{5}, \quad \sin 2\theta = 2\sin \theta \cos \theta = \dfrac{4}{5}$

$\begin{bmatrix} \cos 2\theta & \sin 2\theta \\ \sin 2\theta & -\cos 2\theta \end{bmatrix} = \begin{bmatrix} -\dfrac{3}{5} & \dfrac{4}{5} \\ \dfrac{4}{5} & \dfrac{3}{5} \end{bmatrix}$

2.4   Combining transformations

(a)   **If P has position vector $\begin{bmatrix} 2 \\ 3 \end{bmatrix}$, what is its image P' where $P' = Y(P)$?**

(b)   **What is the matrix for the transformation Y?**

(c)   **How can the position vector of P' be obtained by a simple matrix multiplication**

(a) $\begin{bmatrix} 2 \\ 3 \end{bmatrix} \rightarrow \begin{bmatrix} -2 \\ 3 \end{bmatrix}$ (b) $Y = \begin{bmatrix} -1 & 0 \\ 0 & 1 \end{bmatrix}$

(c) $\begin{bmatrix} -1 & 0 \\ 0 & 1 \end{bmatrix} \begin{bmatrix} 2 \\ 3 \end{bmatrix} = \begin{bmatrix} -2 \\ 3 \end{bmatrix}.$

(a)   **What single transformation is equivalent to Y followed by Q?**

(b)   **What is the matrix for this equivalent transformation?**

(c)   **How is this matrix related to the matrices for Y and Q?**

(d)   **With position vector $\begin{bmatrix} 2 \\ 3 \end{bmatrix}$ for P, find the position vector of P'' by matrix multiplication.**

(a)   Reflection in $x + y = 0$

(b) $\begin{bmatrix} 0 & -1 \\ -1 & 0 \end{bmatrix}$

(c) $QY = \begin{bmatrix} 0 & -1 \\ 1 & 0 \end{bmatrix} \begin{bmatrix} -1 & 0 \\ 0 & 1 \end{bmatrix} = \begin{bmatrix} 0 & -1 \\ -1 & 0 \end{bmatrix}$

(d) $\overrightarrow{OP''} = \begin{bmatrix} 0 & -1 \\ -1 & 0 \end{bmatrix} \begin{bmatrix} 2 \\ 3 \end{bmatrix} = \begin{bmatrix} -3 \\ -2 \end{bmatrix}$

> **(a)** Why is it logical to let QY mean Y first, then Q, contrary to the order in which the expression is read?
>
> **(b)** What does YQ mean?
>
> **(c)** Find the image of *P* under YQ.
>
> **(d)** Does YQ = QY?

(a) **Y**(*P*) can be read as '**Y** acting on *P*' and **QY**(*P*) can be read as '**Q** acting on **Y**(*P*)' It is therefore sensible to take **Y** as acting on *P* to give *P′*, **then Q** as acting on *P′*.

(b) **YQ** means '**Q** first then **Y**'.

(c) (2, 3) $\xrightarrow{\textbf{Q}}$ (−3, 2) $\xrightarrow{\textbf{Y}}$ (3, 2).

(d) **YQ** is a reflection in $y = x$ and **QY** is a reflection in $y = -x$. They are **not** equal.

Exercise 2

1. (a) $X = \begin{bmatrix} 1 & 0 \\ 0 & -1 \end{bmatrix}$ $Y = \begin{bmatrix} -1 & 0 \\ 0 & 1 \end{bmatrix}$ $XY = \begin{bmatrix} -1 & 0 \\ 0 & -1 \end{bmatrix} = YX$.

   (b) Yes, $XY = YX$.

   (c) $XY = YX$ represents a half turn, centre (0, 0).

2. (a) $M = \begin{bmatrix} 0 & 1 \\ 1 & 0 \end{bmatrix}$, $Q = \begin{bmatrix} 0 & -1 \\ 1 & 0 \end{bmatrix}$, $MQ = \begin{bmatrix} 1 & 0 \\ 0 & -1 \end{bmatrix}$, $QM = \begin{bmatrix} -1 & 0 \\ 0 & 1 \end{bmatrix}$

   (b) $MQ \neq QM$

   (c) **MQ** is a reflection in the *x*-axis; **QM** is a reflection in the *y*-axis.

3. (a) $S_1 S_2 = \begin{bmatrix} 1 & 0 \\ 0 & 1 \end{bmatrix} = S_2 S_1$. S_2 is the **inverse** of S_1.

   (b) $S_1 S_3 = \begin{bmatrix} 2 & 1 \\ 1 & 1 \end{bmatrix}$, $S_3 S_1 = \begin{bmatrix} 1 & 1 \\ 1 & 2 \end{bmatrix}$. The combination of shears is not necessarily commutative.

2.5   Inverse transformations

Exercise 3

1. (a) $|A| = 7$, $\quad A^{-1} = \begin{bmatrix} \frac{5}{7} & -\frac{4}{7} \\ -\frac{2}{7} & \frac{3}{7} \end{bmatrix}$

   (b) $|B| = 2$, $\quad B^{-1} = \begin{bmatrix} \frac{1}{2} & \frac{1}{2} \\ -\frac{1}{2} & \frac{1}{2} \end{bmatrix}$

   (c) $|C| = -8$, $\quad C^{-1} = \begin{bmatrix} \frac{3}{8} & \frac{1}{8} \\ \frac{1}{4} & -\frac{1}{4} \end{bmatrix}$

2. (a) The determinant is 1 for both matrices.

   (b) They are shears.

   (c) The area is unchanged so the area factor is 1, the determinant.

   (d) $\begin{bmatrix} 1 & -2 \\ 0 & 1 \end{bmatrix} \begin{bmatrix} 1 & 0 \\ 3 & 1 \end{bmatrix} = \begin{bmatrix} -5 & -2 \\ 3 & 1 \end{bmatrix}$ The determinant of the product is 1.

   (e) Area of image is 1.

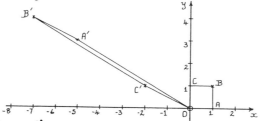

2.6   Linear transformations

> (a) If a is the position vector of a general point, what can you say about the points λa, where λ is any real number?
>
> (b) Show that $T(\lambda a) = \lambda T(a)$ for a general matrix T.
>
> (c) What is the significance of this result?

(a) All points λ **a** lie on a straight line through $(0, 0)$, parallel to **a**.

(b) $T(\lambda \, a) = \begin{bmatrix} p & q \\ r & s \end{bmatrix} \begin{bmatrix} \lambda x \\ \lambda y \end{bmatrix} = \begin{bmatrix} p\lambda x + q\lambda y \\ r\lambda x + s\lambda y \end{bmatrix} = \lambda \begin{bmatrix} px + qy \\ rx + sy \end{bmatrix} = \lambda \begin{bmatrix} p & q \\ r & s \end{bmatrix} \begin{bmatrix} x \\ y \end{bmatrix} = \lambda \, T(a)$

(c) Any point on the line through $(0, 0)$ parallel to **a** is mapped onto a point on the line through $(0, 0)$ parallel to **T** (**a**). Straight lines through the origin are therefore mapped onto straight lines through the origin.

What happens to the square grid under the transformations given by these matrices?

(a) $A = \begin{bmatrix} 1 & 0 \\ 0 & 1 \end{bmatrix}$;

(b) $B = \begin{bmatrix} 2 & -1 \\ -4 & 2 \end{bmatrix}$

(c) $C = \begin{bmatrix} 0 & 0 \\ 0 & 0 \end{bmatrix}$.

(a) The grid is unchanged.

(b) The grid is squashed onto the single line $y = -2x$.

(c) $\begin{bmatrix} 0 & 0 \\ 0 & 0 \end{bmatrix}\begin{bmatrix} x \\ y \end{bmatrix} = \begin{bmatrix} 0 \\ 0 \end{bmatrix}$. The grid is squashed onto the single point $(0,0)$.

Which of the following transformations are linear and which are non-linear? In each case justify your answer.

(a) Rotations about the origin.

(b) Translations.

(c) $\begin{bmatrix} x \\ y \end{bmatrix} \rightarrow \begin{bmatrix} x^2 \\ y \end{bmatrix}$

(d) $\begin{bmatrix} x \\ y \end{bmatrix} \rightarrow \begin{bmatrix} x + y \\ x - y \end{bmatrix}$

(a) A rotation about $(0, 0)$ can be described by a matrix $\begin{bmatrix} \cos\theta & -\sin\theta \\ \sin\theta & \cos\theta \end{bmatrix}$ and so is linear.

(b) A linear transformation satisfies

$$T(0 \times a) = 0 \times T(a) \quad \text{i.e.} \quad T(0) = 0$$

The only translation which is linear is the identity transformation.

(c) $\begin{bmatrix} 1 \\ 1 \end{bmatrix} \rightarrow \begin{bmatrix} 1 \\ 1 \end{bmatrix}$, $\begin{bmatrix} 2 \\ 3 \end{bmatrix} \rightarrow \begin{bmatrix} 4 \\ 3 \end{bmatrix}$ and $\begin{bmatrix} 1 \\ 1 \end{bmatrix} + \begin{bmatrix} 2 \\ 3 \end{bmatrix} = \begin{bmatrix} 3 \\ 4 \end{bmatrix} \rightarrow \begin{bmatrix} 9 \\ 4 \end{bmatrix} \neq \begin{bmatrix} 1 \\ 1 \end{bmatrix} + \begin{bmatrix} 4 \\ 3 \end{bmatrix}$

so the transformation is **not** linear.

(d) $\begin{bmatrix} x+y \\ x-y \end{bmatrix} = \begin{bmatrix} 1 & 1 \\ 1 & -1 \end{bmatrix}\begin{bmatrix} x \\ y \end{bmatrix}$ so the transformation is linear.

3   *Simultaneous equations*

3.1   Introduction

> **Give an algebraic solution of**
>
> $$x + 2y = 5 \qquad ①$$
> $$x - y = 2 \qquad ②$$

Algebraic methods involve eliminating one variable to produce an equation for the other variable. The most efficient method of eliminating a variable is usually that of adding or subtracting various multiples of the equations:

$① - ②,$

$$3y \; = \; 3$$
$$\Rightarrow \quad y \; = \; 1$$

In $①,$

$$x + 2 = \; 5$$
$$\Rightarrow \quad x \; = \; 3$$

Or

$① + 2②,$

$$3x \; = \; 9$$
$$\Rightarrow \quad x \; = \; 3$$

In $①,$

$$3 + 2y \; = \; 5$$
$$\Rightarrow \quad y \; = \; 1$$

Exercise 1

1. Let (x,y) be the coordinates of C.

$$\begin{bmatrix} 1 & -4 \\ 2 & 1 \end{bmatrix} \begin{bmatrix} x \\ y \end{bmatrix} = \begin{bmatrix} 6 \\ 3 \end{bmatrix}$$

$$\begin{bmatrix} x \\ y \end{bmatrix} = \begin{bmatrix} 1 & -4 \\ 2 & 1 \end{bmatrix}^{-1} \begin{bmatrix} 6 \\ 3 \end{bmatrix} = \frac{1}{9} \begin{bmatrix} 1 & 4 \\ -2 & 1 \end{bmatrix} \begin{bmatrix} 6 \\ 3 \end{bmatrix} = \frac{1}{9} \begin{bmatrix} 18 \\ -9 \end{bmatrix} = \begin{bmatrix} 2 \\ -1 \end{bmatrix}$$

$$C = (2, -1)$$

2. $\quad 2x - y = a \qquad\qquad 6 - (-2) = a \qquad\quad a = 8$
    $\quad x + 4y = b \qquad\qquad 3 + 4\,(-2) = b \qquad\; b = -5$

3. $\quad y = x + 5 \;\Rightarrow\; -x + y \; = 5 \qquad\qquad ①$
    $\quad 2y = 5 - 3x \;\Rightarrow\; 3x + 2y = 5 \qquad\qquad ②$

$3① + ②,$

$$5y = 20$$
$$\Rightarrow \quad y \; = 4$$

In $①,$

$$x \; = -1 \text{ and } D \text{ is } (-1,4)$$

3.2 Geometrical ideas

> **(a)** What difficulty arises when solving these equations with algebraic methods?
>
> **(b)** What geometrical property do you notice?
>
> **(c)** Describe what happens as a varies.

(a) If these equations are solved by elimination, the equation $a = 5$ is obtained. For other values of a the equations cannot be solved.

(b) The equations represent parallel lines.

(c) As a increases from 5, the line moves away from the line of $2x + 3y = 5$ in the direction of the positive axes, whilst remaining parallel to it.

Similarly, as a decreases from 5, the line moves away in the direction of the negative axes, whilst remaining parallel.

Exercise 2

1. $s + 2t = 3$ and $4t = 5 - 2s$ have no solution since they represent parallel lines, and therefore have no point of intersection. This can be seen by rearranging one of the equations:

$$4t = 5 - 2s \Rightarrow 2s + 4t = 5 \Rightarrow s + 2t = 2.5$$

This should be compared with the other equation, $s + 2t = 3$

2. (a) Any pair of equations such that $\dfrac{a_2}{a_1} \neq \dfrac{b_2}{b_1}$

   (b) Any pair of equations such that $\dfrac{a_2}{a_1} = \dfrac{b_2}{b_1} \neq \dfrac{c_2}{c_1}$

   (c) Any pair of equations such that $\dfrac{a_2}{a_1} = \dfrac{b_2}{b_1} = \dfrac{c_2}{c_1}$

3. (a) $a = \dfrac{-3}{b} \neq 2$. For example, $a = 6$, $b = -0.5$

(b) $a = 2$, $b = -1.5$

(c) $ax + 3y = 4$ \qquad ①

$x - by = 2$ \qquad ②

① $- a$ ②, $(3 + ab)\,y = 4 - 2a \Rightarrow y = \dfrac{2\,(2 - a)}{ab + 3}$

b ① $+ 3$ ②, $(ab + 3)\,x = 4b + 6 \Rightarrow x = \dfrac{2\,(2b + 3)}{ab + 3}$

(d) The lines are parallel if $a = \dfrac{-3}{b}$

3.3 Crushing transformations

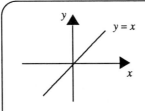

By considering a number of points, check that the image space for

$$\begin{bmatrix} 2 & 3 \\ 2 & 3 \end{bmatrix}$$

is the line $y = x$

$$\begin{bmatrix} x' \\ y' \end{bmatrix} = \begin{bmatrix} 2 & 3 \\ 2 & 3 \end{bmatrix}\begin{bmatrix} x \\ y \end{bmatrix} = \begin{bmatrix} 2x + 3y \\ 2x + 3y \end{bmatrix} \quad \text{and so } y' = x'$$

Check that the image of any point on the line $3y = 5 - 2x$ is $(5, 5)$.

$$\begin{bmatrix} 2 & 3 \\ 2 & 3 \end{bmatrix}\begin{bmatrix} x \\ y \end{bmatrix} = \begin{bmatrix} 2 & 3 \\ 2 & 3 \end{bmatrix}\begin{bmatrix} x \\ \frac{5-2x}{3} \end{bmatrix} = \begin{bmatrix} 2x + 5 - 2x \\ 2x + 5 - 2x \end{bmatrix} = \begin{bmatrix} 5 \\ 5 \end{bmatrix}$$

3.4   Elimination

> **Explain how the solution set depends upon the value of a.**

Substituting $x = 2$ and $y = 1$ in ③ gives $a = 6 - 5 = 1$.

If $a = 1$, the solution is $x = 2$, $y = 1$.

If $a \neq 1$, the solution set is empty.

> **(a)   Why is the solution not unique ?**
>
> **(b)   How would a third equation affect the situation ?**

(a)   The solution is not unique because x and y both depend on z and z may take any value.

(b)   A third equation might give a unique solution, by fixing the value of z.

> **Why choose to eliminate x first ?**

Any of the three variables can be eliminated first, but x has equal coefficients in equations ② and ③, thus making the elimination simpler.

Exercise 3

1. $x - 3y + z = -2$ ①

     $2x + 2y - z = 7$ ②

     $x - 5y + 3z = -6$ ③

     ① − ③, $2y - 2z = 4 \Rightarrow y - z = 2$ ④

     ② − 2③, $12y - 7z = 19$ ⑤

     12④ − ⑤, $-5z = 5$

              $\Rightarrow z = -1$

     In ④, $y = 1$

     In ①, $x = 2$

     $x = 2$, $y = 1$, $z = -1$

2. $7x - y + 4z \quad = 4$ ①

    $2x + 5y - 3z \quad = 23$ ②

    $6x - 2y + 5z \quad = -4$ ③

    $5$① $+$②, $37x + 17z = 43$ ④

    $2$① $-$ ③, $8x + 3z = 12$ ⑤

    $17$⑤ $- 3$④, $25x = 75$

    $x = 3$

    In ⑤ $z = -4$

    In ① $y = 1$

    $x = 3,\ y = 1,\ z = -4$

3. $x + y + z + t = 3$ ①

    $-x + y - z + 2t = 5$ ②

    $x - 3y + z - t = -5$ ③

    $4x + y - 2z + t = 9$ ④

    ① $+$ ②, $2y + 3t = 8$ ⑤

    ① $-$ ③, $4y + 2t = 8$ ⑥

    etc.

The solution is $x = 1,\ y = 1,\ z = -1,\ t = 2$.

4. (a) $2x - y + 7z = 5$ ①

    $3x + 4y + 2z = 2$ ②

    $5x - 3y + 2z = 13$ ③

    $3x - 2y + z = a$ ④

    ② $-$ ③, $-2x + 7y = -11$ ⑤

    $7$② $- 2$①, $17x + 30y = 4$ ⑥

    etc.

    $x = 2,\ y = -1,\ z = 0$ is the solution of ① , ② and ③ .

    (b) In ④ , $a = 6 - (-2) + 0 = 8$.

3.5   Planes

How many different configurations of three planes can you find ?

Ignoring cases where two or more of the planes are parallel, there are just three configurations.

A.   One pair of planes intersect along a line and the third cuts across this. Thus the three planes intersect at a single point.

The sloping planes which form the roof of the porch intersect to form a line. This intersects the plane of the wall at a single point.

B.   All three planes intersect at a common line. This configuration is called a sheaf.

The roof, the wall and the floor of the attic have a common line.

C.   The planes intersect, in pairs, along three parallel lines. The three planes have no common point. This configuration is called a prism.

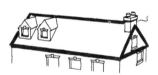

The two planes of the roof and the floor of the attic form a hollow prism.

How can you recognise when planes are parallel from their equations?

Two lines

$$a_1x + b_1y = c_1$$
$$a_2x + b_2y = c_2$$

are **parallel** if $\dfrac{a_1}{a_2} = \dfrac{b_1}{b_2} \neq \dfrac{c_1}{c_2}$.   They are the **same** if $\dfrac{a_1}{a_2} = \dfrac{b_1}{b_2} = \dfrac{c_1}{c_2}$.

Similarly, two planes

$$a_1x + b_1y + c_1z = d_1$$
$$a_2x + b_2y + c_2z = d_2$$

are **parallel** if $\dfrac{a_1}{a_2} = \dfrac{b_1}{b_2} = \dfrac{c_1}{c_2} \neq \dfrac{d_1}{d_2}$. They are the **same** if $\dfrac{a_1}{a_2} = \dfrac{b_1}{b_2} = \dfrac{c_1}{c_2} = \dfrac{d_1}{d_2}$.

Exercise 4

1. $3x - y + 4z = 4$ ①

    $2x + 3y - 2z = -15$ ②

    $2x - 4y + z = 1$ ③

    ① $- 4$③ , $-5x + 15y = 0$

    ② $+ 2$③, $6x - 5y = -13$

    This leads to $x = -3, y = -1, z = 3$.

2. $2x - 5y + 3z = 3$ ①

    $3x + 2y - 5z = -5$ ②

    $5x - 22y + 17z = 17$ ③

    $2$② $-3$① , $19y - 19z = -19$

    $2$③ $-5$① , $-19y + 19z = 19$

    The last two equations are the same and therefore consistent. For any values of
    y and z such that $y = z - 1$, a value of x can be found from ①. The equations
    have infinitely many solutions

    $$x = -1 + \lambda, \quad y = -1 + \lambda, \quad z = \lambda \quad \text{for any value of } \lambda.$$

    The three planes form a sheaf.

3. $x + y - z = 0$ ①

    $3x - 4y - z = 9$ ②

    $5x - 2y - 3z = 15$ ③

    ③ $-$② $-2$① , $0 = 6$

    This is not possible, so there is no solution. Since no pair of planes is parallel, the
    three planes form a hollow prism.

4. Eliminating x and z from the equations gives

    $$(a - 12)y = 3b$$

    (a) The three planes intersect at the single point $(4, 1, -6)$.

    (b) There are infinitely many solutions,

    $$x = \frac{1}{5} (19 - 2\lambda) , \quad y = \lambda , \quad z = \frac{1}{5} (-38 + 29\lambda), \text{ for any value of } \lambda.$$

    The planes form a sheaf.

    (c) The equations are incompatible and have no solution. The three planes have
    no common point of intersection. Since none of the planes are parallel, they
    form a hollow prism.

4 Identifying transformations

4.2 Fixed directions

> **(a)** For a fixed direction, is the choice of eigenvector unique?
>
> **(b)** Can two parallel eigenvectors have different eigenvalues?

(a) Any vector in the appropriate direction can be taken as an eigenvector.

(b) The eigenvalue is the same regardless of the choice of eigenvector in that direction.

Exercise 1

1. $\begin{bmatrix} 0 & -1 \\ 6 & 5 \end{bmatrix}\begin{bmatrix} -1 \\ 3 \end{bmatrix} = \begin{bmatrix} -3 \\ 9 \end{bmatrix} = 3\begin{bmatrix} -1 \\ 3 \end{bmatrix} \quad \begin{bmatrix} 0 & -1 \\ 6 & 5 \end{bmatrix}\begin{bmatrix} 1 \\ -2 \end{bmatrix} = \begin{bmatrix} 2 \\ -4 \end{bmatrix} = 2\begin{bmatrix} 1 \\ -2 \end{bmatrix}$

   The matrix represents a two-way stretch of factors 3 and 2 in directions $\begin{bmatrix} -1 \\ 3 \end{bmatrix}$ and $\begin{bmatrix} 1 \\ -2 \end{bmatrix}$

2. $\begin{bmatrix} 8 & 10 \\ -5 & -7 \end{bmatrix}\begin{bmatrix} 2 \\ -1 \end{bmatrix} = \begin{bmatrix} 6 \\ -3 \end{bmatrix} = 3\begin{bmatrix} 2 \\ -1 \end{bmatrix} \quad \begin{bmatrix} 8 & 10 \\ -5 & -7 \end{bmatrix}\begin{bmatrix} -1 \\ -1 \end{bmatrix} = \begin{bmatrix} -18 \\ 12 \end{bmatrix} \neq \lambda\begin{bmatrix} -1 \\ -1 \end{bmatrix}$

   $\begin{bmatrix} 8 & 10 \\ -5 & -7 \end{bmatrix}\begin{bmatrix} 1 \\ -1 \end{bmatrix} = \begin{bmatrix} -2 \\ 2 \end{bmatrix} = -2\begin{bmatrix} 1 \\ -1 \end{bmatrix} \quad \begin{bmatrix} 8 & 10 \\ -5 & -7 \end{bmatrix}\begin{bmatrix} -2 \\ 3 \end{bmatrix} = \begin{bmatrix} 14 \\ -11 \end{bmatrix} \neq \lambda\begin{bmatrix} -2 \\ 3 \end{bmatrix}$

   $\begin{bmatrix} 2 \\ -1 \end{bmatrix}$ and $\begin{bmatrix} 1 \\ -1 \end{bmatrix}$ are eigenvectors.

   The matrix represents a two-way stretch of factors 3 and –2 in directions $\begin{bmatrix} 2 \\ -1 \end{bmatrix}$ and $\begin{bmatrix} 1 \\ -1 \end{bmatrix}$.

3. $\begin{bmatrix} 0 & 1 \\ 1 & 0 \end{bmatrix}$ is a reflection in $y = x$ and so $\begin{bmatrix} 1 \\ 1 \end{bmatrix} \rightarrow \begin{bmatrix} 1 \\ 1 \end{bmatrix}, \begin{bmatrix} 1 \\ -1 \end{bmatrix} \rightarrow \begin{bmatrix} 1 \\ 1 \end{bmatrix}$.

   $\begin{bmatrix} 0 & 1 \\ 1 & 0 \end{bmatrix}\begin{bmatrix} 1 \\ 1 \end{bmatrix} = \begin{bmatrix} 1 \\ 1 \end{bmatrix}, \quad \begin{bmatrix} 0 & 1 \\ 1 & 0 \end{bmatrix}\begin{bmatrix} 1 \\ -1 \end{bmatrix} = \begin{bmatrix} -1 \\ 1 \end{bmatrix} = -\begin{bmatrix} 1 \\ -1 \end{bmatrix}$

4.3 Finding eigenvalues

Exercise 2

1. (a) $(3 - \lambda)(2 - \lambda) - 2 = 0$ $\qquad$ (b) $(-2 - \lambda)(-5 - \lambda) + 2 = 0$

   $\lambda = 1, 4$ $\qquad\qquad\qquad\qquad$ $\lambda = -4, -3$

   (c) $(2 - \lambda)(6 - \lambda) - 12 = 0$ $\qquad$ (d) $(0.75 - \lambda)(-0.5 - \lambda) + 0.25 = 0$

   $\lambda = 0, 8$ $\qquad\qquad\qquad\qquad$ $\lambda = -0.25, 0.5$

4.4 Finding eigenvectors

Exercise 3

1. (a) $\begin{bmatrix} 1 \\ -1 \end{bmatrix}, \begin{bmatrix} 2 \\ 1 \end{bmatrix}$

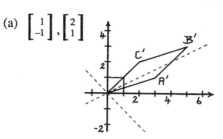

(b) $\begin{bmatrix} 1 \\ -1 \end{bmatrix}, \begin{bmatrix} 2 \\ -1 \end{bmatrix}$

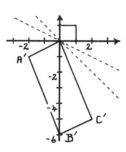

(c) $\begin{bmatrix} 3 \\ 2 \end{bmatrix}, \begin{bmatrix} 1 \\ -2 \end{bmatrix}$

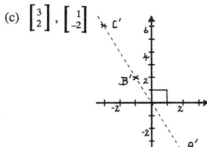

(d) $\begin{bmatrix} 1 \\ 2 \end{bmatrix}, \begin{bmatrix} 2 \\ 1 \end{bmatrix}$

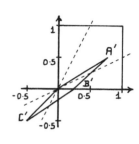

4.5 Diagonal matrices

Exercise 4

1. (a) $\lambda = 3, -2$

Eigenvectors $\begin{bmatrix} 1 \\ 1 \end{bmatrix}, \begin{bmatrix} 1 \\ -4 \end{bmatrix}$

(i) $\mathbf{M} = \begin{bmatrix} 1 & 1 \\ 1 & -4 \end{bmatrix} \begin{bmatrix} 3 & 0 \\ 0 & -2 \end{bmatrix} \begin{bmatrix} 0.8 & 0.2 \\ 0.2 & -0.2 \end{bmatrix}$

(ii) Two way stretch of factors 3 and −2 in directions $\begin{bmatrix} 1 \\ 1 \end{bmatrix}$ and $\begin{bmatrix} 1 \\ -4 \end{bmatrix}$.

(b) $\lambda = 2, -5$

Eigenvectors $\begin{bmatrix} 3 \\ 1 \end{bmatrix}, \begin{bmatrix} 1 \\ -2 \end{bmatrix}$

(i) $\mathbf{M} = \begin{bmatrix} 3 & 1 \\ 1 & -2 \end{bmatrix} \begin{bmatrix} 2 & 0 \\ 0 & -5 \end{bmatrix} \begin{bmatrix} \frac{2}{7} & \frac{1}{7} \\ \frac{1}{7} & -\frac{3}{7} \end{bmatrix}$

(ii) Two way stretch of factors 2 and −5 in directions $\begin{bmatrix} 3 \\ 1 \end{bmatrix}, \begin{bmatrix} 1 \\ -2 \end{bmatrix}$.

(c) $\lambda = 7, -5$

Eigenvectors $\begin{bmatrix} 1 \\ 1 \end{bmatrix}, \begin{bmatrix} 1 \\ -1 \end{bmatrix}$

(i) $\mathbf{M} = \begin{bmatrix} 1 & 1 \\ 1 & -1 \end{bmatrix} \begin{bmatrix} 7 & 0 \\ 0 & -5 \end{bmatrix} \begin{bmatrix} 0.5 & 0.5 \\ 0.5 & -0.5 \end{bmatrix}$

(ii) Two way stretch of factors 7 and -5 in directions $\begin{bmatrix} 1 \\ 1 \end{bmatrix}, \begin{bmatrix} 1 \\ -1 \end{bmatrix}$.

(d) $\lambda = \dfrac{1}{2}, \dfrac{1}{3}$

Eigenvectors $\begin{bmatrix} 2 \\ 1 \end{bmatrix}, \begin{bmatrix} 3 \\ 2 \end{bmatrix}$

(i) $\mathbf{M} = \begin{bmatrix} 2 & 3 \\ 1 & 2 \end{bmatrix} \begin{bmatrix} \frac{1}{2} & 0 \\ 0 & \frac{1}{3} \end{bmatrix} \begin{bmatrix} 2 & -3 \\ -1 & 2 \end{bmatrix}$

(ii) Two way stretch of factors $\dfrac{1}{2}$ and $\dfrac{1}{3}$ in directions $\begin{bmatrix} 2 \\ 1 \end{bmatrix}, \begin{bmatrix} 3 \\ 2 \end{bmatrix}$.

2. Eigenvectors $\begin{bmatrix} 1 \\ 3 \end{bmatrix}, \begin{bmatrix} 2 \\ -1 \end{bmatrix}$.

$$\mathbf{U} = \begin{bmatrix} 1 & 2 \\ 3 & -1 \end{bmatrix} \qquad \mathbf{D} = \begin{bmatrix} \frac{1}{3} & 0 \\ 0 & 2 \end{bmatrix}$$

$$\mathbf{M} = \begin{bmatrix} 1 & 2 \\ 3 & -1 \end{bmatrix} \begin{bmatrix} \frac{1}{3} & 0 \\ 0 & 2 \end{bmatrix} \begin{bmatrix} \frac{1}{7} & \frac{2}{7} \\ \frac{3}{7} & -\frac{1}{7} \end{bmatrix} = \begin{bmatrix} \frac{1}{3} & 4 \\ 1 & -2 \end{bmatrix} \begin{bmatrix} \frac{1}{7} & \frac{2}{7} \\ \frac{3}{7} & -\frac{1}{7} \end{bmatrix} = \begin{bmatrix} \frac{37}{21} & -\frac{10}{21} \\ -\frac{5}{7} & \frac{4}{7} \end{bmatrix}$$

4.6 Transition matrices

How can you determine what is likely to happen

(a) during the next few days;

(b) in the long term?

(a) If today is sunny, the input matrix is $\begin{bmatrix} 1 \\ 0 \end{bmatrix}$, so the probability that tomorrow will be sunny is $\mathbf{T} \begin{bmatrix} 1 \\ 0 \end{bmatrix}$

The probability matrix for two days time will be $\mathbf{T} \left(\mathbf{T} \begin{bmatrix} 1 \\ 0 \end{bmatrix} \right) = \mathbf{T}^2 \begin{bmatrix} 1 \\ 0 \end{bmatrix}$

(b) In general, the probability matrix for n days time will be $\mathbf{T}^n \begin{bmatrix} 1 \\ 0 \end{bmatrix}$. The behaviour in the long term is investigated on Tasksheet 5.

4.7 Inverse matrices

Show that any eigenvector is of the form $k \begin{bmatrix} 1 \\ 0 \end{bmatrix}$.

Suppose $\begin{bmatrix} 1 & 1 \\ 0 & 1 \end{bmatrix} \begin{bmatrix} x \\ y \end{bmatrix} = \lambda \begin{bmatrix} x \\ y \end{bmatrix}$, for $\begin{bmatrix} x \\ y \end{bmatrix} \neq \mathbf{0}$.

Then $\begin{vmatrix} 1-\lambda & 1 \\ 0 & 1-\lambda \end{vmatrix} = 0 \Rightarrow (1-\lambda)^2 = 0 \Rightarrow \lambda = 1$.

So $\begin{bmatrix} 1 & 1 \\ 0 & 1 \end{bmatrix} \begin{bmatrix} x \\ y \end{bmatrix} = \begin{bmatrix} x \\ y \end{bmatrix} \Rightarrow x+y = x \Rightarrow y = 0$.

Hence $\begin{bmatrix} x \\ y \end{bmatrix} = k \begin{bmatrix} 1 \\ 0 \end{bmatrix}$

(a) Show that the characteristic equation of

$M = \begin{bmatrix} 4 & -5 \\ 1 & -2 \end{bmatrix}$ is

$\lambda^2 - 2\lambda - 3 = 0$.

(b) Find $M^2 - 2M - 3I$.

(c) Comment on your answers to parts (a) and (b).

(a) $\begin{vmatrix} 4-\lambda & -5 \\ 1 & -2-\lambda \end{vmatrix} = 0$

$\Rightarrow (4-\lambda)(-2-\lambda) + 5 = 0$

$\Rightarrow \lambda^2 - 2\lambda - 3 = 0$

(b) $M^2 - 2M - 3I = \begin{bmatrix} 11 & -10 \\ 2 & -1 \end{bmatrix} - \begin{bmatrix} 8 & -10 \\ 2 & -4 \end{bmatrix} - \begin{bmatrix} 3 & 0 \\ 0 & 3 \end{bmatrix} = \begin{bmatrix} 0 & 0 \\ 0 & 0 \end{bmatrix}$

(c) The matrix satisfies its own characteristic equation.

This result is investigated on Tasksheet 6.

5 Numerical techniques

5.1 Gaussian elimination

> Show that $x_2 = 3$

$$1.25 x_2 - 3.25 x_3 = -2.75$$
$$\Rightarrow \quad 1.25 x_2 - 6.5 = -2.75$$
$$\Rightarrow \quad 1.25 x_2 = 3.75$$
$$\Rightarrow \quad x_2 = 3$$

Exercise 1

1.

Operation	x_1	x_2	x_3	c	Row No.
	8	2	4	26	①
	4	5	−1	0	②
	2	−3	5	22	③
② $-\frac{1}{2}$①	0	4	−3	−13	④
③ $-\frac{1}{4}$①	0	$-\frac{7}{2}$	4	$\frac{31}{2}$	⑤
⑤ $+\frac{7}{8}$④	0	0	$\frac{11}{8}$	$\frac{33}{8}$	⑥

$x_3 = 3,\ x_2 = -1,\ x_1 = 2$

2. (a)

Operation	x_1	x_2	x_3	c	Row No.
	9	5	−3	11	①
	5	3	2	6	②
	3	−8	1	1	③
② $-0.\dot{5}$①	0	$0.\dot{2}$	$3.\dot{6}$	$-0.\dot{1}$	④
③ $-0.\dot{3}$①	0	$-9.\dot{6}$	2	$-2.\dot{6}$	⑤
⑤ $+43.5$④	0	0	161.5	−7.5	⑥

$x_3 = -0.05,\ x_2 = 0.27,\ x_1 = 1.06$ (2 decimal places)

(b)

Operation	x_1	x_2	x_3	c	Row No.
	4.56	−7.59	2.61	0.67	①
	1.52	5.77	4.30	9.72	②
	0.57	9.84	2.24	5.45	③
② $-\frac{1}{3}$①	0	8.30	3.43	9.50	④
③ $-\frac{1}{8}$①	0	10.79	1.91	5.37	⑤
⑤ $-1.3$④	0	0	−2.55	−6.98	⑥

$x_3 \approx 2.74,\ x_2 \approx 0.01,\ x_1 \approx -1.40.$

5.2 LU decomposition

Exercise 2

1. $\mathbf{LU} = \begin{bmatrix} 1 & 0 & 0 \\ 2 & 1 & 0 \\ 0 & -1 & 1 \end{bmatrix} \begin{bmatrix} 3 & -2 & 2 \\ 0 & 2 & 0 \\ 0 & 0 & 1 \end{bmatrix}$

$\begin{bmatrix} 1 & 0 & 0 \\ 2 & 1 & 0 \\ 0 & -1 & 1 \end{bmatrix} \begin{bmatrix} 14 \\ -8 \\ 0 \end{bmatrix} = \begin{bmatrix} 14 \\ 20 \\ 8 \end{bmatrix}$

$\begin{bmatrix} 3 & -2 & 2 \\ 0 & 2 & 0 \\ 0 & 0 & 1 \end{bmatrix} \begin{bmatrix} 2 \\ -4 \\ 0 \end{bmatrix} = \begin{bmatrix} 14 \\ -8 \\ 0 \end{bmatrix}$

$x_1 = 2, \quad x_2 = -4, \quad x_3 = 0.$

2. $\mathbf{LU} = \begin{bmatrix} 1 & 0 & 0 & 0 \\ \frac{1}{3} & 1 & 0 & 0 \\ \frac{4}{3} & -\frac{1}{2} & 1 & 0 \\ 0 & \frac{3}{2} & -\frac{1}{3} & 1 \end{bmatrix} \begin{bmatrix} 3 & 0 & 1 & -2 \\ 0 & 2 & -\frac{1}{3} & \frac{17}{3} \\ 0 & 0 & \frac{3}{2} & \frac{11}{2} \\ 0 & 0 & 0 & -\frac{17}{3} \end{bmatrix}$

$\begin{bmatrix} 1 & 0 & 0 & 0 \\ \frac{1}{3} & 1 & 0 & 0 \\ \frac{4}{3} & -\frac{1}{2} & 1 & 0 \\ 0 & \frac{3}{2} & -\frac{1}{3} & 1 \end{bmatrix} \begin{bmatrix} 1 \\ \frac{50}{3} \\ 18 \\ -17 \end{bmatrix} = \begin{bmatrix} 1 \\ 17 \\ 11 \\ 2 \end{bmatrix}$

$\begin{bmatrix} 3 & 0 & 1 & -2 \\ 0 & 2 & -\frac{1}{3} & \frac{17}{3} \\ 0 & 0 & \frac{3}{2} & \frac{11}{2} \\ 0 & 0 & 0 & -\frac{17}{3} \end{bmatrix} \begin{bmatrix} 2 \\ 0 \\ 1 \\ 3 \end{bmatrix} = \begin{bmatrix} 1 \\ \frac{50}{3} \\ 18 \\ -17 \end{bmatrix}$

$x_1 = 2, \quad x_2 = 0, \quad x_3 = 1, \quad x_4 = 3.$

5.3   An iterative approach

In Example 3, the number of decimal places recorded in the answer increased at each stage of the iteration. Can you suggest why this is a sensible policy in iterative problems?

The errors in successive iterations gradually reduce and the process of iteration is self correcting. There is little point in recording the first iteration to spurious accuracy, but as the process continues it is necessary to record to a level which reflects the accuracy of the approximation.

Exercise 3

1.   Let $x_0 = 0$, $y_0 = 1$.

$$x_{n+1} = \frac{3-2y_n}{8} \quad \text{and} \quad y_{n+1} = \frac{2x_{n+1}+5}{5}$$

$$x_1 = 0.13 \qquad y_1 = 1.05$$

$$x_2 = 0.113 \qquad y_2 = 1.045$$

...   ...

$x = 0.11$ and $y = 1.05$ (2 decimal places)

[Using a program, $x_{11} \approx 0.113636364$ and $y_{11} \approx 1.04545455$.]

2.   Let $x_0 = 1$, $y_0 - 1$, $z_0 = 1$

$$x_{n+1} = \frac{4+3y_n+z_n}{20} \quad \text{and} \quad y_{n+1} = \frac{8-2x_{n+1}-3z_n}{5} \quad \text{and} \quad z_{n+1} = \frac{11-4x_{n+1}+y_{n+1}}{7}$$

$$x_1 = 0.4, \ x_2 = 0.84, \ x_3 = 1.46286$$

Eventually $x \approx 0.360406091$
$y \approx 0.586294416$
$z \approx 1.44923858$

6 Canonical form

6.1 Kernels

> **If a matrix equation**
>
> $$Ar = b$$
>
> **has two solutions, r_1 and r_2, then show that**
>
> $$r_2 = r_1 + k, \quad k \in \text{Ker}(A).$$

$$A(r_2 - r_1) = Ar_2 - Ar_1$$

$$= b - b$$

$$= 0$$

$\Rightarrow \quad r_2 - r_1 \in \text{Ker}(A)$

$\Rightarrow \quad r_2 = r_1 + k, \quad k \in \text{Ker}(A).$

6.2 Finding kernels

Exercise 1

1. (a) The canonical form is $\begin{bmatrix} 1 & 0 & \frac{1}{7} \\ 0 & 1 & \frac{-5}{7} \\ 0 & 0 & 0 \end{bmatrix}$. The kernel is $\lambda \begin{bmatrix} -1 \\ 5 \\ 7 \end{bmatrix}$, $\lambda \in \mathbb{R}$.

   (b) The canonical form is $\begin{bmatrix} 1 & 0 & \frac{10}{23} \\ 0 & 1 & \frac{-4}{23} \\ 0 & 0 & 0 \end{bmatrix}$. The kernel is $\lambda \begin{bmatrix} -10 \\ 4 \\ 23 \end{bmatrix}$, $\lambda \in \mathbb{R}$.

   (c) The canonical form is $\begin{bmatrix} 1 & 0 & 0 \\ 0 & 1 & 0 \\ 0 & 0 & 1 \end{bmatrix}$. The kernel is $\begin{bmatrix} 0 \\ 0 \\ 0 \end{bmatrix}$.

2. The canonical form is $\begin{bmatrix} 1 & 0 & -3 & 4 \\ 0 & 1 & -6 & 7 \\ 0 & 0 & 0 & 0 \\ 0 & 0 & 0 & 0 \end{bmatrix}$

The kernel is $\lambda \begin{bmatrix} 3 \\ 6 \\ 1 \\ 0 \end{bmatrix} + \mu \begin{bmatrix} -4 \\ -7 \\ 0 \\ 1 \end{bmatrix}$; $\quad \lambda, \mu \in \mathbb{R}$.

3. (a) The canonical form is $\begin{bmatrix} 1 & 0 & \frac{1}{2} & \frac{3}{4} & 3 \\ 0 & 1 & \frac{1}{2} & \frac{1}{4} & 2 \\ 0 & 0 & 0 & 0 & 0 \\ 0 & 0 & 0 & 0 & 0 \end{bmatrix}$

The kernel is $\lambda \begin{bmatrix} -1 \\ -1 \\ 2 \\ 0 \\ 0 \end{bmatrix} + \mu \begin{bmatrix} -3 \\ -1 \\ 0 \\ 4 \\ 0 \end{bmatrix} + \gamma \begin{bmatrix} -3 \\ -2 \\ 0 \\ 0 \\ 1 \end{bmatrix}$; $\quad \lambda, \mu, \gamma \in \mathbb{R}$.

(b) 3 dimensions are lost in applying the transformation **S**.

6.3   General solutions

> **Check the above assertion.**

$$\begin{bmatrix} 1 & -2 & 1 & 5 \\ 2 & 1 & 4 & 9 \\ 3 & -1 & 5 & 14 \end{bmatrix} \quad \begin{matrix} ① \\ ② \\ ③ \end{matrix}$$

$\begin{matrix} ① \\ ② - 2① \\ ③ - 3① \end{matrix}$ $\begin{bmatrix} 1 & -2 & 1 & 5 \\ 0 & 5 & 2 & -1 \\ 0 & 5 & 2 & -1 \end{bmatrix}$ $\begin{matrix} ④ \\ ⑤ \\ ⑥ \end{matrix}$

$\begin{matrix} ④ + \frac{2}{5}⑤ \\ \frac{1}{5}⑤ \\ ⑥ - ⑤ \end{matrix}$ $\begin{bmatrix} 1 & 0 & \frac{9}{5} & \frac{23}{5} \\ 0 & 1 & \frac{2}{5} & -\frac{1}{5} \\ 0 & 0 & 0 & 0 \end{bmatrix}$

Exercise 2

1. (a)

$$x + 3y = 5 \qquad ①$$

$$-2x + 5y = 1 \qquad ②$$

$$4x - 3y = 5 \qquad ③$$

$$① + ③, \quad 5x = 10 \Rightarrow x = 2$$

In $①, \quad y = 1$

These values for x and y satisfy all three original equations. The equations are consistent and have unique solution $x = 2, \quad y = 1$

(b)
$$\begin{bmatrix} 3 & 4 & -1 & 9 \\ 1 & 3 & 3 & 8 \\ 3 & -1 & -11 & -6 \end{bmatrix} \text{ reduces to the canonical form } \begin{bmatrix} 1 & 0 & -3 & -1 \\ 0 & 1 & 2 & 3 \\ 0 & 0 & 0 & 0 \end{bmatrix}$$

The general solution is $\begin{bmatrix} -1 \\ 3 \\ 0 \end{bmatrix} + \lambda \begin{bmatrix} 3 \\ -2 \\ 1 \end{bmatrix}, \quad \lambda \in \mathbb{R}.$

(c)
$$\begin{bmatrix} 1 & 4 & -3 & 1 & 1 & -7 \\ 2 & -1 & 1 & 4 & 1 & 0 \end{bmatrix} \text{ reduces to the canonical form } \begin{bmatrix} 1 & 0 & \frac{1}{9} & \frac{17}{9} & \frac{5}{9} & \frac{-7}{9} \\ 0 & 1 & \frac{-7}{9} & \frac{-2}{9} & \frac{1}{9} & \frac{-14}{9} \end{bmatrix}$$

The general solution is $\begin{bmatrix} \frac{-7}{9} \\ \frac{-14}{9} \\ 0 \\ 0 \\ 0 \end{bmatrix} + \lambda \begin{bmatrix} -1 \\ 7 \\ 9 \\ 0 \\ 0 \end{bmatrix} + \mu \begin{bmatrix} -17 \\ 2 \\ 0 \\ 9 \\ 0 \end{bmatrix} + \gamma \begin{bmatrix} -5 \\ -1 \\ 0 \\ 0 \\ 9 \end{bmatrix}$

2.
$$\begin{bmatrix} 1 & -1 & 0 & 1 & 5 \\ 5 & 2 & -4 & 1 & 4 \\ 2 & 5 & -4 & -2 & -11 \\ 9 & 5 & -8 & 1 & 3 \end{bmatrix} \text{ reduces to the canonical form } \begin{bmatrix} 1 & 0 & \frac{-4}{7} & \frac{3}{7} & 2 \\ 0 & 1 & \frac{-4}{7} & \frac{-4}{7} & -3 \\ 0 & 0 & 0 & 0 & 0 \\ 0 & 0 & 0 & 0 & 0 \end{bmatrix}$$

(a)
$$\lambda \begin{bmatrix} 4 \\ 4 \\ 7 \\ 0 \end{bmatrix} + \mu \begin{bmatrix} -3 \\ 4 \\ 0 \\ 7 \end{bmatrix}; \qquad \lambda, \mu \in \mathbb{R}.$$

(b) Points of the form $\mathbf{r} = \begin{bmatrix} 2 \\ -3 \\ 0 \\ 0 \end{bmatrix} + \lambda \begin{bmatrix} 4 \\ 4 \\ 7 \\ 0 \end{bmatrix} + \mu \begin{bmatrix} -3 \\ 4 \\ 0 \\ 7 \end{bmatrix}; \quad \lambda, \mu \in \mathbb{R}.$